Writing With Spirit

A Journalistic Guide to Effective Writing

A Journalistic Guide
to Effective Writing

Writing with
Spirit

by Lois Sweet

CASTLE QUAY BOOKS
C A N A D A

Writing With Spirit

Copyright © 2003, Castle Quay Books Canada

Cover Design by John Cowie, eyetoeye, design
Copy editing by Audrey Dorsch, Dorsch Editorial
Photo of Lois Sweet by Peter Puxley
Printed by Essence Publishing, Belleville, Ontario

Published by CASTLE QUAY BOOKS
1740 Pilgrim's Way, Oakville ON L6M 1S5
Tel: (416) 573-3249 Fax: (519) 748-9835
E-mail: info@castlequaybooks.com
www.castlequaybooks.com

National Library of Canada Cataloguing in Publication

Sweet, Lois, 1947-
   Writing with spirit : a journalistic guide to effective writing / by Lois Sweet ; with a chapter on media law by Klaus Pohle.

Includes bibliographical references and index.
ISBN 1-894860-21-7

   1. Journalism—Authorship. 2. Reporters and reporting. I. Pohle, Klaus
II. Title.

PN4775.S94 2003   808'.06607   C2003-902891-7

CASTLE QUAY BOOKS
CANADA

For Hannah (Sweet) Moor
who set the bar high

Table of Contents

Acknowledgments

Many people contributed to the making of this book. I am particularly grateful to those who edit and write for the Christian press in this country. They work with integrity, diligence and great commitment to their profession. Despite the many demands on their time and energy, they gave generously to this project. They provided me with copies of their publications and discussed their work at length. They were also endlessly patient when I returned with follow-up questions. Their observations were profound and created a frame on which to build this book. I tried to remain true to their perspectives. Responsibility for any errors or omissions resides solely with me.

My deepest thanks to Harold Jantz, David Harris, Joe Sinasac, Kenn Ward, Doug Koop, Lloyd Mackey, Rick Hiebert, Muriel Duncan, Gail Reid, Ian Adnams, Patria Rivera, Bill Fledderus, Leanne Larmondin, Ted Schmidt and Marianne Meed Ward.

Thanks also to David Napier, Michael McAteer, Bob Harvey, Nancy Lindquist, Debra Fieguth, Chris Pullenayegem, Murray MacAdam, Donna Sinclair, Michael

Swan, John Bird, Laurie McBurney, Laura Ieraci, Tara Oetting, Sister Marie Claire Boucher, Tom Dickey and Mike Milne for their contributions.

Klaus Pohle, my colleague and the author of the chapter on media law, deserves a special thank you. He agreed to contribute even though he was carrying a particularly heavy load at the university. He provided a sympathetic ear during the writing process and was tolerant when I pestered him for copy. His generosity in sharing his expertise in this important area is greatly appreciated.

My colleagues at Carleton University's School of Journalism and Communication were extremely supportive. Special thanks to Barbara Freeman, Catherine McKercher and Roger Bird. Thanks also to adjunct professor John Sawatsky for allowing me to draw on his list of interviewing "sins."

When this book was only an idea in my head, it was Brian Stiller who suggested I turn it into a reality. He helped make that possible by introducing me to Larry Willard, Canadian publisher of Augsburg Fortress Press. Brian believed in me and in the value of a book like this. I appreciate his vote of confidence.

Many thanks to Larry Willard, who took on the book with great enthusiasm. He was a pleasure to work with—committed, professional and with a way of making things happen! It was Larry who induced Audrey Dorsch to take on the task of editing the book. Audrey is in great demand and for good reason; she is one of the best in the business. When I learned that she had agreed to be the editor, I knew everything was going to be just fine. It was an honour to work with her.

During the course of researching and writing, friends Kelly Crichton and Mel Watkins provided welcome meals and respite weekend after weekend. I'm sure they thought the book would never get finished. (And perhaps it wouldn't have without their comforting friendship.)

A special note of gratitude is due to Hannah Moor. When I was young, she proved it is possible to combine creativity with faith. Later I observed her faith in action. When a massive heart attack followed by a series of strokes spelled an end to more than a quarter century of writing, Hannah refused to wallow in self-pity. She found solace in the words, "Beware of harkening back to what you once were, while God is waiting to make of you something that you have never been." And so Hannah, now 80, sought other ways of being. With her sunny disposition, her unerring faith and her gentle compassion for others, she is a source of strength to many, including me.

Finally, as always, I owe so much to my family. To my children, Chinta, Luke and Kate, who buoyed my spirits when the task seemed impossible. To Alison Myers, my daughter-in-law (also a journalist), who shared ideas about "focusing" stories. And to Peter Puxley, my husband, who was, and is, a constant source of strength and love.

L.S.

Preface

I sold my first story when I was 11 years old. It was to a Christian publication in the United States that syndicated stories and poems to churches across North America. My own church was a subscriber and everyone who attended received a copy. Reading it from cover to cover was one of the high points of Sundays. Hannah Moor from Barrie, Ontario, was a fine writer and a regular contributor, so it wasn't unusual to open the paper and see her name.

Hannah Moor was my aunt. I wanted to write like her.

The $6 I got for the story seemed like a fortune then. But it wasn't enough to keep me writing and submitting. Although I couldn't name it, perhaps I sensed that if I were to take writing seriously, then discipline was required—something I hadn't yet developed (and continue to struggle with). There could also have been a not-yet-vocalized fear of failure—a state of mind that dries up the creative juices.

Other barriers? Certainly not enough self-awareness. Insufficient life experience. Lack of a firm enough grounding in my faith or, indeed, enough experience of that faith (making writing about faith feel like a fraudulent act).

And definitely not enough awareness of the writing process or the tools required to be a good writer.

I never dreamed then that I would one day become a professional writer—albeit as a journalist, rather than a writer of fiction. Though the differences between the two are obvious, there are also many similarities. Both attempt to tell the truth about the world as they see it, experience it or try to understand it—although fiction writers exercise a "poetic license" to embellish, embroider and expand on the material they use. Both are interested in ideas—although an essential task of the journalist is to convey abstract ideas concretely.

The best of both use language in a way that entices readers to stay with them, to read through to the end. Often, they are rewarded with an angry, upset or disappointed audience. When people don't like the message, they too often target the messenger. When that happens, it doesn't matter whether you write fiction or journalism; it's not a comfortable position to be in.

Finally, the best practitioners of both care deeply about their work. They love it. It is not just a job; it is a vocation, a calling. They do it because they *have* to. They do it because they are curious about life, are hungry for knowledge, and feel they have something important to say. They do it to stretch themselves. In the process, they change and grow. And if they are good at what they do, they take their readers with them!

Exploring the art of fiction writing is not the focus of this book and, indeed, is beyond the scope of my experience. However, what motivates both types of writers is the desire to communicate. This means writing clearly and writing well.

The idea for this book grew out of a desire to see the principles of journalism applied more strenuously to Christian publications, particularly as they relate to researching and writing. Part of the challenge in writing the book was in recognizing there is no homogeneity in Christian publications. There are literally hundreds across Canada. Some small, some large. Some rural, some urban. Some serve diverse audiences, some cater to specific interest groups. Some seek to challenge their readership to embrace new ideas, to question traditional church authority. Others are viewed as the mouthpiece of traditional church authority.

But all are self-identified Christian publications. For them, this work is "a holy calling," as Doug Koop, editorial director of *ChristianWeek*, put it. The need for thorough researching and fine writing doesn't depend on doctrinal differences. It is essential to them all.

My hope is that this book will be of service to you who write for them.

Introduction

When Jacob Riis, New York editor, briefly considered abandoning journalism for the ministry, a minister friend told him, "No, no, Jacob, not that. We have preachers enough. What the world needs is consecrated pens.

– From *Muckraking:
The Journalism that Changed America,
edited by Judith and William Serrin.*

I love journalism. It's a profession that demands the investigative skills of a detective, the tenacity of a long-distance runner, the compassion and honesty of a saint, the precision of a brain surgeon and the story-telling abilities of a W.O. Mitchell. It's a long list and for good reason. Journalists are guardians of the public interest. We do this by using our researching and writing skills to help people become better informed. When done well, journalism supports the cause of democracy.

Doing it well is the key. This means applying the principles of journalism with diligence and integrity, always attempting to uncover as much about a situation, from as many different perspectives, as possible. It means being in the reality business. This isn't easy. Every day we're assaulted by hundreds, if not thousands, of ads. Every day politicians, marketers, educators, entertainers—you name it—attempt to capture our attention with a perfect sound bite. They have a message to convey, and they want to control it.

Our job is to ferret out as much of the truth about situations and about issues as possible. It isn't to act as messengers for those in positions of power or for the rich and famous. It isn't to rewrite press releases—just another name for propaganda. Instead, we are required to tap into our natural curiosity and to use all of our senses, as well as our intellectual abilities, to come up with fair, accurate and balanced stories that serve the community we write for.

I think of journalism as a mission. However, simply putting "journalism" and "mission" together in the same sentence can be contentious. Many mainstream journalists would be appalled at the association. To them, having a "mission" implies having a hidden agenda, thus making them incapable of doing the job of a professional.

And what are the essentials that characterize a professional? Of course there's the necessity that all stories be accurate, that information be checked and verified before it's published, and that sources be identified. There's the necessity of providing complete and balanced information by fairly presenting the positions of all sides in an issue or a debate. There's the necessity that stories be written well, with brevity and style. Finally—and this is the critical one when it comes to the issue of "mission"—there's the necessity that journalists not inject their own biases and prejudices when researching and writing.

To me, striving to meet those standards on every story we write should be our primary mission. Another part of this mission is to help open the lines of communication between people who hold different perspectives, to enlarge the range of voices being heard on an issue, to expose the values inherent in these various positions and, where possible, to help people find common ground.

However, that's only one way to use the word "mission." The other, of course, is to use it interchangeably with "advocacy." Take the case of a labour reporter named Mary Heaton Vorse. In 1912, after workers went on strike in Lawrence, Mass., she decided to abandon her dream of writing fiction and remain a journalist. "I could do one thing," she said. "I could write. I could try to make other people see what I had seen, feel what I had felt. I wanted to make others as angry as I was. I wanted to see wages go up and the babies' death rate go down."

That became her mission.

Even though they may not refer to what they do in those terms, many of today's secular journalists also have a mission. They may want to expose corruption in high places, unfair business practices, racism, sexism or, once again, you name it. When they do this well it's not because they had an "axe to grind" and found facts to support their position. Instead, it was because they took a complex issue and did the hard work of researching it—layer upon layer—and interviewing people who represented a variety of perspectives. And they did it with an awareness of their own biases. They used their powers of critical thinking to assess how they felt about an issue and then firmly put those feelings aside while they sought "truth." Finally, they were prepared to report whatever they found, even if it ran counter to their worldviews.

Being guided by those principles is how journalists who advocate on behalf of the rights of others, who are on a self-identified "mission," can call themselves professionals. It's also part of the rationale for this book. People who report and write for the Christian press are, unabashedly and unselfconsciously, on a mission. They begin with the premise that belief in the life, death and resurrection of Jesus Christ has the power to change lives. They understand that good communication skills are needed to convey that message. They want to use their writing to make people aware of realities that are important to their faith.

Sometimes there's the false assumption that journalism in the church press should be practiced differently from journalism in the mainstream. But good journalism is good journalism. Writers for Christian publications should follow the same journalistic principles and apply all the skills of other professional writers.

In philosophical terms this means giving voice to the voiceless and heightening awareness on issues that affect people's perception of, and experience of, their faith. In practical terms this means knowing how to identify good story ideas, do thorough research, conduct informative interviews, develop a strong focus, structure an interesting story and use language well.

Reporting and commentary, the two arms of journalism, are just as much a part of articles in church press publications as they are in the secular press. But sometimes writers for the Christian press confuse the two. They might insert opinion in news stories or neglect to do the research necessary for balanced coverage as well as informative analysis and opinion. This creates a challenge for editors struggling to provide top calibre material. It can also create confusion for readers, who have the right to expect accurate and fair news reports as well as insightful and thought-provoking commentary based on more than knee-jerk reactions.

Everything in this book is guided by the presumption that church press publications play an essential and important role in the lives of Christians across the country. For this reason it is particularly essential that the research and writing in those publications represent the height of journalistic excellence. It doesn't matter how honourable your mission, how good your cause; if you can't be relied on to produce professional copy, then your stories will be suspect and your mission could be compromised.

Your job is to speak the truth, even when the truth is painful, even when the reaction may be negative and hurtful to the messenger. This is a job that requires not just professional principles, but courage.

A good journalist can't expect an external reward. There will be times, of course, when people will praise you. But they may also rebuke you, even condemn you. The real reward comes from having delved into a subject and then produced what you believe is an accurate interpretation of an event or issue based on hard work, deliberate thinking and good writing.

There is also the reward of being changed by your work, of growing spiritually and of developing a deeper understanding of your faith.

Sometimes you'll discover that there are no easy answers to the tough issues you'll be covering. As a professional it's important not to stoop to jingoism of any kind or resort to simplistic ideological crutches. Every situation, every issue, should be approached and analyzed as though you are learning about it for the first time. This means coming to those issues with an open mind and not allowing your own biases or perspectives to colour your professionalism.

After researching an issue you might discover that the situation is different from what you initially expected. To me this is part of the pleasure of journalism. You begin with something and then, as you delve deeper and deeper into it, it transforms into something else. This is another reason for approaching every situation, every issue, with an open mind. Without that attitude you could well miss one of the most exciting aspects of your work. And you would not be providing a service to your readership.

This book will provide concrete tools for facing such tasks as generating story ideas and then doing the research essential to ensuring that stories are not just informative but are also accurate and balanced. Chapters will address the arts of observation and interviewing—two indispensable tools. In particular, it will examine the journalistic style of writing. There are a number of ways to describe this style— clear, simple, tight, focused, energetic. But always journalistic writing means writing accurately, armed with solid research methods.

We'll examine the act of writing in three ways. First, we'll look at the various forms journalistic writing takes and explore different approaches to them. Second, we'll explore some of the essential skills required to write well and examine issues of style and grammar. Third, we'll discuss writing as a process—the discipline of writing, the self-discovery of writing, the joy of writing and the headache of writing!

In addition, we'll address the tension that can exist for church press writers who strive to be journalistically professional but who come to those stories with a worldview formed and informed by their faith. We'll also address the tensions that many editors feel between their journalistic sense of professionalism and the demand (implicitly or explicitly) from their organizational leadership to put a positive spin on everything. Sometimes Christian leaders and decision-makers have little idea what constitutes "news." In their haste to paper over differences, to perhaps prevent the mainstream press from learning anything negative about their sensitive issues, they don't necessarily realize that they've crossed an ethical boundary.

Some of the ethical issues facing both editors and writers will be explored in this book. And my colleague, Prof. Klaus Pohle, an expert in media law, will examine how knowledge of the law can inform your writing (and save you grief).

Anyone writing for the church press should recognize that he or she is part of a long and honourable tradition in this country. A lot of the early mainstream press was identified with religious perspectives. And many of the current church press publications have been running for more than a century. They are essential social institutions that attempt through their work to, as one contributor put it, "help define our identity and feed our faith as we journey through life."

By using words effectively, you will be able to impart the passion you feel for the issues, people and faith you care about. Through your stories, people will be challenged to grapple with and discover what it means to be a Christian in Canada today.

Story Ideas
and Research

When Harold Jantz took over as editor of the *Mennonite Brethren Herald* in 1964, he had only three days to work with his predecessor before being on his own. It was a steep learning curve. Jantz was responsible for advertising, circulation and, of course, editorial content. The task was daunting and he wasn't sure exactly how to approach the first issue. He knew he had some solid story ideas. But he also knew that the planning and execution of *everything*—from thereon in—would be totally his responsibility. He asked himself, "Should I use all my story ideas in this first go, or—just to be safe—should I save some for the next edition?"

Jantz threw caution to the wind. "I decided to put all of them into that first edition," he said, "and, you know, I never ran out of ideas. There were always more. In fact, if you're alert to what's going on, there is no shortage of ideas. There are lots and lots of them out there."

What are story ideas? In a nutshell, they are ideas that can be followed up to generate stories of interest to your readers. They can be based on news events. They can be follow-ups to news stories. They can involve questioning popular assumptions. They can be a recapitulation of history as seen through a modern faith perspective. They can use the experience of an individual to generalize on a social condition. They can spring from personal reflections.

One of the most valuable assets for generating story ideas is an innate sense of curiosity. Why did something happen? Why is it happening now? Why is so-and-so taking that position on an issue as opposed to another? What are the implications of this action or position as opposed to that one?

Questioning conventional wisdom can often be a productive way to find stories. But simply following up on your desire to know about something is often the spark required to ignite a story idea.

Everything begins with an idea. The questions that often stymie both writers and editors are where to find them and how to find them. In fact, they're all around us, everywhere— in the people we meet, the things that happen to us and those we know and love, and in what we see, hear and read. However, story potential is one thing. Recognizing that potential is quite another.

Being able to recognize a good story idea when you come upon it depends on a number of factors. First, it's important to know your audience. Who is your readership? What do they need—and want—to know? Second, it's important to know the purpose (or mission statement) of the publication. Does it exist as a conduit for the church hierarchy to impart its message? Or does it attempt to foster discussion and debate among all sectors of the church? What are the strengths and weaknesses of the leadership of your publication? Are people open to having you raise uncomfortable or controversial issues or ideas in print? If so, are they then willing to see the fallout through to the end? If the answer is "no" to both, then what are the limits, and is there *any* elasticity in them?

Finally, it's essential that you know yourself. Do you have what it takes to run with a particular story idea, to do the research required and then capture its essence in your writing and editing?

Christian publications are as diverse, interesting and complex as the people and the faiths they reflect. Some are editorially independent of church leadership and survive by subscriber loyalty, while others serve as organs of their denominations and are financially dependent on them. Some have editorial independence but financial dependence. Then there are those that don't cater to any particular church or denomination but attempt to capture a broad readership of people who are interested in keeping abreast of Christian views and issues generally.

No matter how they're financed or how dependent/independent they are editorially, the bottom line is this: the quality of their story ideas will have a huge effect on their success. In 1993, for example, when Rick Hiebert took over as editor of *Testimony*, a monthly magazine published by the Pentecostal Assemblies of Canada, he found that much of the magazine was "a rehash of sermons from men. I refuse to publish those," he said. "They're written for a different format and don't transpose well into a magazine format. As well, the magazine is meant to be much more than that. It's meant to be a 'voice,' a way for people in the pews to express their opinions."

This means Hiebert has his ear constantly to the ground. In journalistic terms, it's known as "shoe leather reporting" (walking the streets of your "beat" or neighbourhood so consistently you wear down the soles of your shoes). Both terms imply being in touch with the issues and concerns of your readership. In fact, the best in the business identify an issue or concern even before their readers recognize that the issue has significance beyond themselves.

Joe Sinasac took over the editorial helm of the national Catholic newspaper, *The Catholic Register*, after an extensive career in the mainstream press. It's a background that serves him well at the *Register*. "Like any city editor, I'm always watching for what's going on," he said. "I constantly monitor the news. I'm about hard news, so I read four papers a day. I get the New York Times on-line and monitor many religious wire services. I steal ideas all the time. Always I'm on the lookout for 'What does this mean for Catholics?' As a result, our readers are now getting news and information about things they can't get, and aren't getting, anywhere else."

Kenn Ward, former editor of *Canada Lutheran*, a magazine published eight times a year by the Evangelical Lutheran Church in Canada, said he constantly has his antennae out. "I try to read as broadly as I can. I watch newscasts—CBC Newsworld, Vision TV. I travel and I talk to people. It's especially important to be at conventions because that's where a lot of personal contact takes place. That's when people tell me what's going on in their lives."

Being highly visible also works in terms of getting story ideas from potential freelancers or interested readers. Ward said people regularly come up to him and say, "I've got an idea. What do you think about this?" He's there to listen and provide instant feedback.

What's going on in the lives of those who work for Christian publications, or in the lives of their friends, is another sources of story ideas. Then there is the attempt to get readers to identify what's going on in their own lives and either to write about the struggles and issues themselves or be a source in a story.

Muriel Duncan, editor of *The United Church Observer*, a publication for the United Church of Canada, said, "Most of our stories are about the struggles people have to find meaning in their faith and the part that faith plays in their lives and decision-making and how they find God. And, because we're concerned about both the body and the soul, we encourage people to write about the critical points in their lives. The family with the child with the birth defect, for example, or having a teenager in trouble with the law. Some issues cut pretty close to the bone. And sometimes the church doesn't make it easy for people to talk about their disappointments. Writing about them is a connector to others."

ChristianWeek, Canada's bi-weekly national Christian newspaper, has five regional reporters who file a monthly quota of stories. They're the ones with their fingers on the pulse of their regions. They know the communities they cover. They are attuned to the politics, the issues, the social history, and, of course, the people they write about and write for. "And we never have any problem coming up with story ideas," said Doug Koop, editorial director.

Ian Adnams, editor of *The Canadian Lutheran*, the national magazine of the Lutheran Church–Canada, said he tries to "be real and touch people where they're at. My magazine helps people think through their faith and how it applies and touches every aspect of their lives."

So every once in a while he turns to his readers and involves them. (This could be referred to as "interactive" journalism.) For example, when the Harry Potter books hit the youth market in a big way, Adnams sent out a question to the 700 or so people he has on an e-mail list. He asked what they thought of the books considered controversial by many Christians. "Three to one, people were in favour of them," he said. "Then some people got mad because the responses didn't agree with their perspective. So I was accused of not being balanced. But I reflected what's out there."

In another e-mail, he asked, "What does it mean to be an Easter people?" "This is a market-driven approach," explained Adnams. "It gets readers involved and anxious to read the next edition."

But it doesn't matter how great the story idea is if it won't see the light of day. Hiebert said there have been times when editions of *Testimony* have been junked in a church office because the minister didn't want his congregation reading it. (*Testimony* is sent directly to Pentecostal churches, not to individual subscribers.) Yet he believes the magazine's stories should "inspire, instruct or inform. And 'instruct' works both ways," said Hiebert. "I feel strongly about examining what we believe and putting it all under the microscope. Sometimes people feel threatened if another opinion is expressed. But to me it's important to give people that opportunity. I try to get both sides of an issue. I encourage people to be outspoken."

Ward's denomination expects tough issues to be raised. "We wouldn't have a robust faith if we didn't do that," he said. "We recognize we need a spectrum of thought. The church would be offended if issues weren't raised. For example, we did a major story on patenting genes because we thought people needed to understand the issues and see how it is faith-related. Same with homosexuality. That's a tough one, but we covered it fairly."

"However," he added, "I do know that if we just covered that sort of thing, we'd lose our entire subscription base. I'd personally rather cover more of that kind of issue, but the readership isn't there. If you cover such issues too often, they say it's in their face. But if you don't, they say you aren't relevant."

Then, of course, there are the stories that aren't generated by writers or editors but are driven by news. Something happens that is too important to ignore—an event, a doctrinal pronouncement, a criminal charge—and a responsible publication reports it. This can be the source of a lot of discomfort and friction. Covering the issue fairly and accurately takes courage.

"We don't go looking for bad news," said Koop. "But we'll report it and we'll report it fairly when it occurs. This ticks people off. Church culture is very protective and forgiving and private when it comes to those [negative] things.

Unfortunately, numerous times we've had to tell bad news stories. It's an important part of what we do. Our goal isn't to present a false picture of the church. It's to chronicle the engagement of Christians with the world as we live it. This frequently involves struggle and conflict—and it's news."

When he was editor of the *Anglican Journal*, David Harris wrote an award-winning editorial that explored why there is so much bad news in Christian publications. Entitled "Reporting bad news part of Good News message" (Feb. 1999), the editorial pointed out that though the Bible is God's self-revelation to the world, it's full of bad news stories—stories that "have so much graphic violence that in any other context they would be deemed unsuitable for children."

Harris questioned why people get so upset by bad news. To him it's because most people—but especially Christians—want the world to be better. When they're told by their paper that it isn't, their first response is to shoot the messenger. As Harris put it, "The fact is that wishing for a nicer world doesn't make it so. Having the best information possible to help one make the decisions one can make to improve the world is the most anyone can realistically hope for. For Anglicans, that might mean being as informed as possible before voting or acting on church matters at parish meetings, councils or synods."

Responding to the question, Why publish difficult stories?—such as the ongoing debate over homosexuality—Harris argued that writing about the issue "allows more people the chance to participate in discussions that might otherwise be confined to academics, senior bureaucrats and church leaders."

This is a "news you can use" approach. It's a reader's friend and a resource. Such stories don't tell readers how to think, but they do help them understand the position that their church is taking.

Some publications deliberately provoke. Why? Because they consider it both their role and their responsibility to challenge readers to apply the gospel to their daily lives. Ted Schmidt, editor of the *Catholic New Times*, said he thinks not enough Christian publications do that. "Most church press stuff is either 'over the top' or has theology that's passé. Our premise is to operate from a strong theological background. We say, 'There are no religious stories. There are only stories as seen through an incarnational lens.' Our role is to do the best we can to analyze the world for our readers and not get mired down by the 50th anniversary of such and such."

Assuming you know your publication and your readership, the last hurdle to be jumped is to know yourself. Part of knowing yourself is learning to trust your intuitive sense about what constitutes a good story idea. Unfortunately, a nose for a story isn't something one is born with. Instead, it's something that evolves through time, with experience. But it can be fostered through reading a lot and analyzing stories. What works? What doesn't? Why?

So, like Sinasac, read newspapers—lots of them, every day. Like Ward, listen and watch broadcast news every day. Excellent story ideas are to be had by following up on stories in the news—examining an angle not covered, for example, especially as it pertains to the faith perspective of your publication. In fact, try spending some time in a library browsing through newspapers several years back. Most stories were dropped after a couple of days, a week at most. However, they usually haven't gone away. Their impact continues to be felt and there are still faith-related implications.

Talk to people—all kinds of people from all walks of life. Ask questions. Think of everything as story fodder: yourself, your friends, your classmates, your co-workers, your neighbours, their children (and yours), television programs, movies, chat rooms, magazines, books and church functions. Check out news releases from corporations, public agencies and institutions. They're usually keen to inform and can be the source of a lot of newsworthy information. Or they can provide you with useful contacts for related stories you're working on. (Check out http://www.newswire.ca. It's Canada's largest wire network, distributing more than 70,000 news releases a year on behalf of public companies, governments, unions, associations, law enforcement agencies and others.)

And, of course, once you begin reporting/writing, you'll begin to build a reputation. The people you meet and interview can be a steady source of story ideas once they learn to trust your professionalism.

Two Carleton University journalism professors suggest some guidelines for developing a nose for stories. In their book, *The Canadian Reporter*, Catherine McKercher and Carman Cumming underline the need for reporters to take the time to develop ideas systematically. And because not every story idea will work out, they also suggest that reporters work with a number of ideas simultaneously. The formula to use, they suggest, is Q–S–A. Think of a *question* that needs answering. Combine that with a *source* that may be willing to answer it and an *audience* that may be interested in hearing the answer.

Further, they suggest emphasizing ideas that need development. The most fruitful ideas will be those you come to with some knowledge—i.e. research. The reality is that no story idea can stand on its own. Research is required. Journalists use three essential research tools—document searches (including the Internet), observation, and live interviews. For the rest of this chapter, we'll deal specifically with document searches and observation.

Document Research

Thorough research is one of the characteristics of a real professional. Good story ideas, developed through solid research and then written with clarity and style, are what build a reputation. And ultimately a good reputation is *everything*. Readers will come to depend on your work once they learn to trust it. But they are by no means the first test. Before your story reaches an audience, your editor needs to know that your work is trustworthy. This means your editor must be convinced that you've covered all the bases.

Getting to first base is the easiest. That's where you'll find the surface facts. These come from such sources as press releases, handouts and speeches. Getting to second base involves getting your material verified by doing interviews and background research (including document searches and unearthing statistical material, if relevant).

Reaching final base is a creative challenge, and it requires perseverance and hard work. It involves being able to interpret and analyze all your material by examining the significance of an event or issue as well as its causes and consequences. You can accomplish this only if you've done enough research to provide context and interviewed enough people to expose the complexities and nuances natural to most social issues.

Examining issues from a faith perspective is no excuse for laziness or for not making the effort to get your facts straight. Before you make any assertion in your stories, stop yourself and ask, What's my evidence?

There is nothing inherently difficult about any of the research steps, but they do require critical thinking. Definitions of critical thinking abound. In this context it's best to think of critical thinking as using your analytical thought processes in pursuit of understanding as much as possible about a situation. It means seeking insights into the complexities you discover. It means continually drawing inferences from your material. It means doggedly searching for facts and then being open minded about where those facts take you. It means changing your entire approach to a story if the facts don't mesh with your original theme. (One of the most condemnatory things that can be said about a journalist is, "She never let the facts stand in the way of a good story.")

Not every story requires documentary research. Writing spot news, for example, is about exactly that—writing "on the spot" about events as they unfold. But that's the norm for dailies, and most religious publications have the luxury of planning their stories and then having the time to research and write them. This means being able to write stories with context, providing background material and perspectives from a variety of sources. Such research provides substance, verification and, equally important, credibility. But bear in mind that any document is only as good as its source—the person or people who originally researched and wrote those documents. So approach everything with an open mind and a healthy dose of skepticism (not cynicism, skepticism). One inaccuracy can damage your credibility enormously—a risk a true professional is not prepared to take.

Much of what you gather will need verification. This is simply another word for checking out the facts to make sure that what you're writing is true. Verification can come about through direct observation, where possible. Where it isn't possible, verification will depend on statistical data from a credible source: documents, reports, books or some kind of physical evidence. (An anecdote is not verification. It's one person's "take" on a story—interesting, but merely hearsay. However, if several people can confirm the details, then you've got the best of both worlds: a good story *and* a true story.)

Today it's almost second nature for young researchers to turn to the Internet for information. Certainly there is a wealth of material available on it. And it's nothing if not convenient. But never, never jump to the conclusion that the Internet is 100 percent reliable. I once heard a librarian refer to the Internet as "one vast uncatalogued library"—like "looking for a needle in a haystack," she said. And anyone who's used the Internet as a research tool knows how right she is. Material is not updated daily, weekly or even monthly. It's not well indexed and it certainly isn't comprehensive. There is no quality control. In fact, what often drives Web sites are the egos and interests of the Web page creators, and they're as fallible as the rest of us.

The librarian who spoke so critically about the Internet also maintained that what you don't know *can* hurt you. People with a particular axe to grind don't necessarily include information contrary to the position they hold. In addition, often missing from the Internet is supporting documentation—tables, graphs and footnotes.

Finally, despite its convenience, the Internet can also mean more work because of the need to double-check information. The only case in which this isn't necessary is when the originator of the site is absolutely credible. Anything on Statistics Canada's official Web site, for example, doesn't need to be double-checked. You can assume its accuracy.

Professionals understand the necessity and value of doing solid research. Unfortunately, the converse has been noticed. Bill Fledderus, senior editor at *Faith Today*, said one of the things that most strikes him about new writers is how seldom they pay attention to research. "They want to tell the story of one person's ministry, or of an event, or profile an institution," he said. "But they don't know how to conceptualize, or where to seek out contextual information that helps readers evaluate their chosen topic."

The irony, he added, is that "many want to write for national publications. But they don't know how to situate an event or ministry story in a national context by using national statistics, by researching to see if there are parallels for their chosen topics in other provinces, for example. I often have to direct writers to people from other parallel programs, to critics, and to other pundits who can say something to help readers evaluate the importance of the writer's chosen topic."

Beginning to research

When you're trying to figure out where to begin, think first of all about what you will need to know. Clearly, background is important. What's been published that might be relevant to your issue? In journalistic terms, this is known as "checking the clips." Begin with your own publication. But also check the databases of other publications, including the mainstream media. Documentary research can be done, of course, at libraries. Magazine articles, books, newspaper clippings and journal articles are all grist for the mill. And don't forget that statistics can provide useful insights.

And then, of course, you need to think about who to interview from organizations, churches and/or interest groups (people who represent both sides of an issue). Then, simply think in terms of getting the five Ws and H answered (who, what, when, where, why and how). But always think context. Facts by themselves don't necessarily tell people a lot. Joe Sinasac, for example, said he always tries to ensure that his readership understands the history of an issue.

"It's the context that explains why things happen," he said. "Why did bishops do nothing in the 1980s when they knew sexual abuse was occurring in the church? Well, what we understand from history is that the best advice they got from psychologists was that pedophilia could be cured. To understand issues, you need to understand the context of the times. And you need to understand context within an entire society, not just within the context of the church."

To that end Sinasac published dozens of stories related to the sexual abuse scandal in the U.S. Each time, the stories examined the complexity of the issue by providing context as well as a Canadian perspective. "We hope to reveal facets to stories that don't usually find their way into the secular press," he said.

Another important thing to think about while researching—and one that doesn't tend to get enough attention in either the religious or the mainstream press—is diversity. Of course it's important to seek diversity of opinion or perspective. You want your stories to be both accurate and thought provoking. But how hard did you work to find people who genuinely reflect the diversity of your readership? Christians are young, old, male, female, able-bodied, disabled, and from a wide variety of ethnic groups. This, too, should be reflected in the stories you write.

Finally, when researching, it helps to ask yourself the following questions: How representative was that source? Do I have a variety of perspectives? Have I interviewed enough people? Do I have the evidence to support my theme? Do I have the micro information (anecdotes, details) that will breathe life into my story? Do I have the macro information (the material that will put the anecdotal information into context)? And finally, Will my research withstand criticism?

Researching documents: A case study

My father was the only member of his family to leave the Soviet Union in 1923. He was a young 21-year-old, his widowed mother's right hand since he was the eldest unmarried son at home. But he was also in love with my mother, and because her family had made a firm decision to come to Canada, he faced a terrible dilemma: stay with his mother and care for her farm with two much younger single brothers, or leave them and follow my mother. He chose to follow my mother. Only days before mother's family left for Canada, they were engaged, and later that year, in Laird, Sask., they were married.

– Excerpted from Harold Jantz's moving story
"A Legacy of Suffering: One Story Among Many,"
first published in the Mennonite Brethren Herald, June 9, 2000.

Between 1923 and 1937 Jantz's grandmother and her children wrote approximately 200 letters to his father and mother in Canada. In them they describe the religious, economic and political repression they suffered in the Soviet Union. The letters are a faithful record of both the horrors lived through and the religious conviction that sustained many of them, especially his grandmother. But for Jantz they represent much more than one family's memorabilia.

"Collectively, the history of the Mennonites in Russia is very important to our churches," wrote Jantz, "both for those who have a Russian/German Mennonite background and for those of other ethnic backgrounds who have entered into this legacy by spiritual birth. What our spiritual ancestors suffered should not be forgotten."

And so Jantz decided to use the letters as a way of depicting a larger social condition. This was a formidable task; almost all were written in a gothic style of German and on whatever kind of paper was available. Many were barely decipherable. Painstakingly, Jantz and family members transcribed about two-thirds of them.

From the letters he learned how an active Mennonite Brethren community was virtually destroyed, how even the singing of Christian songs could get people reported to authorities and how they were robbed of their church. This, combined with famine, disease and the forced exile of family members, caused excruciating pain.

Jantz said he grew up listening to stories about that experience. He remembers sitting between his parents while traveling home from an outing and they would sing, in German, a song about a wanderer who was asked why he doesn't go home. "I have nowhere to go," ran the verse. "I have no home." "They were thinking of their lost Russian home," said Jantz.

As he grew older, he felt drawn to learn more about that experience. But, inveterate researcher that he is, Jantz broadened the scope of his inquiry. He read extensively about the suffering of the Mennonite people in Russia. This helped provide historical context.

He also traveled there and taped 15 hours of the story of the one surviving son of his grandmother. And he interviewed and taped stories of cousins who were part of several of the families of his father's siblings. In addition he transcribed interviews he'd done with his father.

It was an immense amount of material to cull through and synthesize. But for Jantz it was a way of redeeming the suffering—not just of his family, but of the tens of thousands of others of Russian/German Mennonite background who experienced similar oppression. Telling the story was also a way of exposing the power of faith and the presence of God, even in those terrible conditions.

The letters, history books, live interviews and visits to the country (observation) were the research tools Jantz employed. In addition he used his analytical skills to extrapolate meaning. He concluded the award-winning article with observations about the legacy of this experience.

What has the suffering done within our family? It must be said, first, that it has left deep scars. There has been great loss. I have one cousin who lost both parents and all siblings....

The suffering also brought about a deepening. Answers are not as glib. Assurances that God solves all problems are not said as easily. No one who has pleaded, wept and cried to God as my grandmother said she did and felt that heaven seemed as impenetrable as iron can ever be glib about the promises of God.

The suffering brought compassion, too. Compassion for others who've been victims of oppression. Compassion for those who are hounded and despised because their politics don't fit or their colour isn't the one favoured by the government. Compassion for the starving. Compassion for refugees and the stateless....

And, in the end, there remained a bedrock faith in God....

Researching a series: A case study

In 1999 writer David Napier had never heard of residential schools. That's when he was approached by David Harris. The Anglican church was just beginning to deal with the legal ramifications of alleged sexual abuse of Aboriginal children in church-run residential schools. The first court case was heard in 1998 and the judgment came down a year later. The court ruled against the Anglican church. In fact, there was no question of guilt, only of liability. How much would the church have to pay?

Harris, himself an ordained Anglican priest, knew that many Anglicans were confused. They were also anxious. They found it hard to believe that such abuses had taken place within their schools. They wanted the truth—about what happened and the implications for the future of their church. The secular media weren't doing anything of conscquence (other than reporting that court cases were taking place). He said he felt he had no choice but to pursue the issue.

"I wanted a reporter to go out and find out what she or he could with no editorial constraints, and with no view of what to find," said Harris. "I felt it had to be done so that the church could consider what it needed to do."

So he scraped together the money and approached Napier about researching and writing a 10,000-word series on the findings.

It was when they met for lunch that Napier confessed his ignorance of the issue. So Harris gave him an "Indian Residential Schools 101" lesson. Napier was intrigued. But he was also concerned. What if he found that bad things had, indeed, happened in Anglican-run schools? Would the *Anglican Journal* refuse to run with his findings if they were damning? Harris told him that his job was to search for the truth. That, he told Napier, is what readers want to know.

Reassured, Napier accepted the writing challenge. And what a challenge it was! He was given approximately six months to research and write the series. Within that time, he would have to travel the country, interviewing people and searching archives. It was hard to know where to begin.

"First thing I did was to research how native people communicate," said Napier. "I spent two months at that. What I learned was that it is a story-based culture and that things move in circuitous routes. I learned that I'd have to have a lot of patience and not to expect clipped answers. I thought I'd have to be prepared to have the story come full circle." In fact, he said that at one point in his research process, "a native person was walking past me on the street and saw my reading material. He said, 'Be careful. This will haunt you.' And it was true. The people I met had a huge effect on me."

Napier read everything he could get his hands on—academic texts, journal articles, sociological studies. And then he read everything again, just to make sure he understood it all. He also scoped out archives—the Anglican, Presbyterian, Methodist archives, as well as the National Archives in Ottawa and provincial archives in B.C. and Quebec.

He knew, though, that what he needed most wouldn't be found in documents. "I wanted to get to the point where individuals, former teachers, members of churches and people who'd been sexually and emotionally abused, would tell their stories—where their stories would be the story," he said. "And that was the hard part." In fact, this was the first time many of the people he interviewed had ever told anyone what had happened to them.

Napier interviewed approximately 50 people. His objective was to get a range of stories and then tell them with as much balance as possible. He found sources through a variety of means. For example, after reading academic books, he'd contact the authors and, in the course of discussing their findings, would ask if they could suggest people he might interview. He was also fortunate that members of the Aboriginal Healing Foundation Fund were traveling the country, alerting people to the fact that money was available for healing, should they meet eligibility requirements. Napier flew to one of the meetings in Thunder Bay and simply approached people who attended.

Word-of-mouth was another good way to get names of potential interviewees. "It was like pulling on a string," said Napier. "You'd yank it, get a name, then another and another, and only then would you realize how long it was."

Once having obtained a name, he'd phone to set up an interview. "But a call out of the blue can be surprising and disruptive," said Napier, "so I'd introduce myself, explain what I was doing, and say I'd like to call them back to discuss it—if they thought that was appropriate. Lives were at stake, so I wanted everyone to have the opportunity to think about it."

Napier also made it clear that what they said to him would be "on the record," that once he turned on the tape recorder, they were giving him the right to publish their story.

"I never badgered people. I always gave everyone the opportunity to say, 'No.'"

(Very few people who said they'd been abused in residential schools turned him down. But he had little luck getting convicted abusers to talk. He contacted their lawyers, the jails in which they were incarcerated, even wrote letters. All to no avail.)

Before entering a community, he would call the band leader, as a matter of courtesy, to let them know he was coming. Once the leader turned him down cold. Napier said she told him that she'd "get him" if he dared to show up. Her position was that reporters have no regard for people's lives, no stake in the repercussions.

He then phoned the person he'd arranged to interview and asked if he still wanted to meet. "The guy said, 'Yes, come to my office. This isn't her jurisdiction.' He had made up his mind to talk, even though he had never spoken of what had happened to him before and even though his band leader was opposed. I was always aware of how much I was asking of people to talk about their experiences, and of how writing about the issue was going to affect so many people."

When Napier finally finished researching, he was faced with the formidable task of figuring out how to assemble it. So he organized a filing system. He said he used a lot of sticky paper to put papers and notes up on his walls. He also used different colours of pens and paper to be able to see, at a glance, how he'd organized different sections of research.

"It was helpful to see names and key words on a big wall of paper," he said. "But I was also dealing with decades and decades of time. It was at that point that I was just trying to get an outline. I had so many facts. And I was miserable to be around because I was so consumed by it all. It was by far the biggest piece of research I've ever done."

What helped a lot, he said, was to approach the task like a kid with a Grade 8 history essay assignment. "Just get an outline to work from," he kept telling himself. "I knew I had to boil it [the interviews and documents] down, so I could build it up again."

In a very real sense that's exactly what's involved for everyone researching and writing a story—whether it's a 10,000-word series or a 500-word article. Do the research (document searches, interviews and observation), then synthesize the material according to the focus of your piece, adjusted according to what you have learned in the research process. Then let the writing begin!

Napier's series, "Sins of the Fathers" ran as a special section in the May 2000 edition of the *Anglican Journal*. Not only did his research reveal the extent of the abuse at church-run schools, but he uncovered files in the national archives indicating that some Aboriginal children may have been used for experiments involving dental care and dietary changes. This story was picked up by CBC radio, Toronto media outlets, including the *National Post* and *The Globe and Mail*, as well as the *New York Times*.

To this day it's difficult to assess the effect. Harris was offered a buy-out a few months after the series ran. "I think, for the hierarchy, it was too much, too soon," said Harris. "But for the church in general, I believe that some years from now, when someone goes back and reviews that situation, they'll acknowledge that the series helped wake up Anglicans to the fact that some really bad things did happen.

"Not that everyone was bad, or that no good was done," added Harris. "But at that time most people thought that just one or two people had been hurt. 'Sins of the Fathers' explained the criminal activity and the systemic effect that it had. The series helped the scales fall from their eyes."

Observation as a research tool

Probably the first thing that comes to mind when you hear the word "observation" is seeing or watching. Certainly that's an important aspect of what this word means as applied to the journalistic process, but it isn't the only one. In fact, observation requires using all one's sensory faculties—eyes, ears, nose, hands (touch) and sometimes even taste.

Why bother with observation, though, when such concrete tools as document searches are available? Well, because good observation skills enhance credibility. Being able to describe a scene in minute detail reassures readers on two counts. First, if a writer is able to get even the smallest detail right, then readers gain confidence in that person's ability to capture the big picture as well. (The converse is also true: get a minute detail wrong or spell a name incorrectly and it doesn't matter how good everything else is; all will be in doubt.)

The second reason good observation skills enhance credibility is because it's through the details that readers know you were there. It's a way of telling them that what they are reading is not something you got second- or third- or even fourth-hand but that you saw it with your own eyes, heard it with your own ears. It's an important form of verification.

Good observation skills are essential for other reasons, as well. For one thing, good observation can lead to good questions—more on that in Chapter 2. Good observation can also help you write better. Words, after all, often represent images, and many images come from observation. When you move into the writing stage, you'll find that the better your information and the better your detail, the easier the writing becomes.

Just as identifying good story ideas is a learned skill, so is being a good observer. A professional observer doesn't observe randomly but does so purposefully—seeking the telling detail, the incongruent gesture or relationship, attempting to make sense of what he or she sees. Your job is to work at understanding what you see so you can convey this as accurately and concisely as possible to people who weren't there to see it for themselves.

Melvin Mencher, a former journalism professor at Columbia University, has developed some guidelines for becoming a better observer. First, know your community. What is it that your readers need and want to know? Carry that understanding around with you always and it will help you to intuitively know what to look for. Second, try to discover the focus, or theme, of your story as soon as possible. Once you have your focus, you can gather material that supports it—allowing you to ignore the inessentials (and there are always lots of inessentials). Details, after all, must serve a purpose. If they don't, then all they do is clutter your copy.

Finally, he said, keep an eye open for the dramatic, the unexpected. Observation works best if you keep *all* your senses open and alert *all* of the time. This means following what's happening, looking for cause and effect, noting the outcome, and taking down details that will help you explain it all.

Summing up: Why good research matters

It's no exaggeration to say that your reputation can be made or broken on the quality of your research. If you become known as someone who consistently gives your readers a complete, fair and accurate account of what you are covering, then you will have gained the trust of your readership. This is no small accomplishment. However, if you become known as someone who manipulates facts to fit your theme, or who ignores facts altogether to achieve a desired result, you will not be trusted or read. Regaining trust will be a long, difficult, if not impossible, task.

But it isn't just your own reputation that's on the line every time you embark on a new story. There is also the reputation of your editor, your publication and ultimately even your organization or denomination. Everyone will be tainted by association. Perhaps the worst repercussion of all is that inaccurate stories can hurt the people you write about.

In addition, your publication may be the periodical of record for your denomination or church. For years to come people will turn to it for research purposes. They will assume that everything in it is as true and accurate as possible. Should you be in error, it could be picked up and repeated in the future. Even if a correction is run in the following edition, later researchers could miss it. (Corrections are notoriously small.) Error, then, can be compounded by error.

The best way to ensure accuracy and precision is to do solid research. It's also essential to handling fallout from a controversial story. If you *know* you covered all the bases. If you *know* you checked and double-checked sources, then you and your editor will be able to stand up to opposition or criticism. It means there won't be any surprises. You'll be in the best position to defend your work. No more could be asked of you.

But how much research is enough research? That's the $64,000 question. In part, time determines how much research you can do. There's never enough of it. Few publications have the resources or the editorial will to give a writer six months to research and write a 10,000-word series. Instead, the deadline is yesterday. The best thing to do under those circumstances is to think hard about what is both essential and possible, and then scramble to do it. Though document searches may initially be time consuming, it is one of those things that get easier the more time you spend learning to navigate libraries, archives or databases.

Remember, just one more interview or one more document search could make the difference between a passable story and a memorable one, between an accurate story and a skewed one.

I always knew I'd done enough research when new sources were covering ground I'd already trod. Or when they were recommending documents I'd already read. But the final judge was always my own inner voice. Were all the questions I had about the issue answered to my satisfaction? Were all the bases covered? It was the voice that told me I now had enough material to begin the process of digging through it, synthesizing it and then capturing it in a language and a way that would inform and, hopefully, enlighten, my readers.

The Art of the Interview

Facing the press is more difficult than bathing a leper.

– Mother Teresa (1910–1997),
former leader of the Order of
Missionaries of Charity

One of the most interesting, personally satisfying and potentially insightful ways to get information is through an interview. It almost seems unnecessary to describe one. After all, on a daily basis we're inundated by "talking heads" on television and radio—people interviewing other people. And when we read a newspaper, we know instinctively that the quotations used in those stories probably came from an interview. But what is an interview, really, and how can you get the most out of one?

An interview often looks like a simple conversation between two people—and, of course, at one level that's exactly what it is. At another level, though, it's anything but. An interview is actually a contrived situation in which one person is encouraged to open up and talk while the other person prods, explores and records what the first is saying. Questions are asked, answers are given, and facts and ideas are bandied about. What can be difficult for you, the interviewer, to remember is that the person front and centre on stage is *not* the one asking the questions!

Though it may look easy, conducting a good interview is actually hard work. It is also a calculated process. Perhaps it's for that reason many people aren't keen to be interviewed. They worry about being "set up," manipulated or having their words taken out of context. Most people are only too aware of a "Gotcha" mentality, seemingly endemic to the competitive rush of pack journalism. (Which may help explain Mother Teresa's attitude toward the media.) "Gotcha" journalists are known for attempting to set up situations that will trick or confuse their sources into saying something they didn't mean to say, or they will ask questions related to one subject and associate them with another.

Ultimately the worst of "Gotcha" journalism undermines a source's credibility and/or sensationalizes or trivializes an issue or story.

For their part, journalists who write for both the religious and mainstream press worry about being manipulated, getting half-truths or having their professionalism questioned if they accept a source's perspective too readily, too quickly, too unquestioningly. They know their credibility is on the line with each story they write. Their objective, of course, is balance and accuracy.

Without doubt, getting information from an interview can be problematic. People rely on their memories to answer questions, and memory is all too often very selective—and seldom complete. And, of course, it's only natural that people bring their assumptions, values and perspectives to what they are describing, a reality that the professional takes into account when doing an interview.

People may honestly believe that what they are saying is the truth, the whole truth and nothing but the truth. But they are, after all, only human and no one has 100 percent recall. Your job is to try to get the whole picture, not merely a piece of it.

So what does all this mean? First, it means that no single interview is likely to provide you with all the information you need, or with information that is totally accurate. That means doing a number of interviews with people who can offer a variety of accounts and/or perspectives. Second, it means learning interviewing techniques to get as much substance as possible out of all your interviews. Finally, it means that you must be much more than simply a faithful scribe or recorder of information. You must learn to evaluate the information you get from an interview.

Interviews get you to the "meat" of a story. Document searches can provide considerable content. But they seldom provide the life, colour and substance that you get from interviews. *Real* people telling *real* stories about their *real* experiences move you to the heart of an issue. But to get there you should never go into an interview "cold" (i.e. having done no research) unless circumstances absolutely make it unavoidable. Put another way, go into every interview having done preliminary research and having sketched out the kinds of questions you need answered.

When done well, interviews will provide you with the emotional material that will draw readers into your story and, hopefully, even cause them to identify with the subject.

Ultimately, the success of an interview depends on your ability to ask good questions and then to listen well to the answers. You can take a variety of steps to make this process work well and to ensure that the information you glean is as accurate and informative as possible.

Setting up the interview

Under ideal conditions, you'll be able to make interview arrangements in advance. You'll call your potential source.

You'll identify yourself as a writer with such-and-such a publication. You'll tell the person about the story you're working on and why you want to interview him or her for it. You'll then ask if the person would be willing to meet with you, suggesting how much time you think the interview will take. If the source agrees, you'll set up a mutually agreeable time and place (ideally, a site that reveals something about the person— home or office). *And*, just before hanging up, you'll ask if the person can recommend any material you can read in advance to help you prepare for the interview.

That's the ideal. Unfortunately, the ideal is seldom realized. Instead, you may phone to set something up only to discover that the only time available is right now! So have your notepad and pen handy, your tape recorder ready to plug into the phone—and make sure you've done enough preliminary research to have some questions prepared.

Other times you'll be at an event and will interview people on the spot. Or you may have to conduct an interview by e-mail. This is the least desirable option as it prevents you from asking spontaneous follow-up questions and deprives you of the ability to observe. What's more, you won't have the opportunity to establish a rapport. Then there's always the possibility that e-mail answers may have been carefully crafted by a committee.

Regardless of the format, you should follow the basic ground rules of identifying yourself, telling people why you want to talk to them, what you want to talk to them about and approximately how long it will take. Do try to find out, in advance, when the busiest time of the day is for them so you aren't competing for their attention. And, if possible, try to interview them in person in their homes. That's usually where people are most at ease and their environment will tell you quite a bit about them. (An additional benefit is that they may also give you more time.) The worst-case scenario is to have to catch people "on the fly"—between classes, before a speech.

And finally, just because you tell people you're writing an article for such-and-such publication doesn't mean they'll automatically understand that what they say is on the record. So spell that out when dealing with those who are unfamiliar with media practices.

Preparing for the interview

Every interview needs background research. Approach every interview prepared, ready to ask good questions that will get you good answers. Ultimately, you'll need four kinds of answers. You'll need your sources to describe, explain, confirm or deny something. But you can't possibly know what you're going to need from them unless you do preliminary research.

This means consulting with your editor, talking to colleagues, checking the clips, doing documentary research, following up on reading material recommended by your sources. Work with that material and jot down potential questions as you go along. If you're dealing with a professional, get a copy of the person's curriculum vitae. Then follow through on what you learn from it. It will help you to piece together a lot of information before you've asked the first question. It will also give you the full title and correct spelling of the name.

Kenn Ward, former editor of *Canada Lutheran*, said he's learned to take out a couple sheets of paper and write down every question that seems remotely related to the subject he'll be writing about. "It really helps your mind work," he said. "And it shows where you need to do more homework."

Think of *yourself* as a valuable resource. Evaluate through the lens of a professional all the material you get. This will help you find the answers to the questions your readers have about a story. Remember, you are their eyes and ears. As their representative, you need to prepare in a way that will serve them best.

No matter how much research you've done for an interview, however, getting the answers you need requires asking the right questions of the right people.

Who to interview

Who you need to interview depends very much on the nature of your story. Is it a straight news story? In that case, you're probably going to need three sources who can provide you with details, context and reaction. Is it a feature? Then you're going to need a wide spectrum of sources who can both explain or describe an issue, speak to its complexities and provide a range of opinion. If it's a profile, then you're not only going to want to do an extensive interview with the person being profiled, but you'll want to seek out a wide range of people who know that person (family, friends, priest or minister, co-workers, people whose lives have been touched by that person).

Whatever the story, though, it's essential to find the best spokespeople possible. Most editors have huge Filofaxes where they keep names and numbers of sources, filed under particular specialties or subject areas (e.g. Christian ethics, gender relations, Old Testament scholar, contemporary Christian music). But bear in mind that it's never too soon to start your own tracking system. Having names and numbers at your fingertips is an invaluable resource. The sources for earlier stories may help in identifying appropriate sources for another story. (Needless to say, they'll be more cooperative if their experience with you was positive.)

If a news story is generated by a press release, the names and numbers of designated spokespeople will be provided. However, always attempt to broaden the scope of your story.

A press release will tell you the message that the organization or person wants to impart. But you will want to tell your readers what it means, and what the implications are. For that, look for additional people to comment—people with no vested interest in, or direct relationship to, the event or issue in question, but who have some knowledge of the subject.

Whenever possible, try to interview people who are not necessarily "authorities" in a particular area. People in positions of authority or power are obviously an essential element of many stories. They provide leadership and direction and often can contribute biblical interpretation. But what humanizes a story, and what ultimately makes it relevant to readers, is when you relate an issue or an event to their lives. What does it mean to them? What effect is it going to have on them or on those they love? This means talking to people affected by the policy or directive or issue.

For example, in the March–April 2003 edition of *The Catalyst*, a publication of Citizens for Public Justice (www.cpj.ca), Chris Pullenayegem, CPJ's refugee issues coordinator, wrote about the changes Canada has made to the refugee claimant process. His intro to "Candle flickers for asylum seekers at the border" humanizes what could have been a bureaucratic article.

> Having managed through complex routes to make her way to the Quebec-New York state border, Mari looked forward eagerly to reaching the Canadian immigration office at Lacolle. It was, she had been told, the doorway to a new life of security in a country of compassion. Unlike her husband and children, she had escaped being murdered. Her bruised body and broken teeth, though, were grim reminders of the torture she had endured in her home country in Africa. Making a refugee claim would be the first step in a new future.

Imagine Mari's horror when, on reaching the border, she was turned away. As of January, Canadian immigration officers must complete the "front-end" screening process before a refugee claimant is allowed into Canada. This includes fingerprinting, photographing, interviewing, copying documents, checking databases and completing forms. New instructions from Ottawa give our immigration officers more authority to send possible refugee claimants back to the U.S. to await processing.

So having being fingerprinted, photographed, and asked questions, Mari was given a date for an appointment for her claim to be assessed, and told to go back to the States until then. When found by U.S. settlement workers the next day, Mari was in a state of shock, having spent the night in a bus station....

Dealing with reluctant sources

Marianne Meed Ward, former managing editor of *Faith Today*, said she often ran into resistance when trying to get information. It came in two forms. One was from church officials who were wary of media getting information they considered sensitive. "The attitude was often, 'You have no right to know this,'" she said. "But to me, it's my denomination and it's our public I'm writing for. I'd ask whether that person was giving this information to their congregation. I'd say everyone has a right to that information."

The other form of resistance came from people who had been through something painful or exceedingly private. They'd be reluctant to share information, arguing it was too difficult to talk about. In that case, Meed Ward would simply talk with them about their dilemma. "I'd try to point out to them that, although their situation was difficult or painful, what they were going through was actually something that could be of enormous help to others. It could either help others avoid a similar situation, or could help them handle it. I'd point out that we're a family and we need to share our stories and support one another."

Regardless of the root of the reluctance, Meed Ward would explain that her intention was not to make the person look bad; nor was she scandal-mongering. "More often than not," she said, "I needed to explain the positive benefit to be had from imparting bad news. I needed to educate people about why it was important to get this information out."

What Meed Ward had going for her—and what is essential for anyone serious about choosing this work for a profession—is that she knew *why* she was doing what she was doing. She believes it's essential that all the facets of any debate or issue be brought before people so they can make up their own minds.

"I put in [*Faith Today*] masthead Acts 17:11," she said. (The New International Version reads: *Now the Bereans were of more noble character than the Thessalonians, for they received the message with great eagerness and examined the Scriptures every day to see if what Paul said was true.*)

"That verse imparts the notion that accepting all of what someone says as true—in this case, it was Paul—isn't honouring that person, your faith, or God," explained Meed Ward. "It's the idea that it's important to bring together accurate information on the issues we struggle with, to present the pros and the cons, to see if what the person says is true. But ultimately, it's about people deciding for themselves.

"To me," she added, "it's much better to have all the ideas out there, battling them out, than to have them repressed."

Without doubt, there will be times when you will encounter people you need to interview who won't welcome the free and open exchange of ideas. For one reason or another they'll attempt to shut down discussion before it begins. One of the most effective ways of doing this is to bully the interviewer. You might find yourself in a situation in which your loyalty to your church—even to God—will be questioned. Or your intelligence might be challenged, or you find yourself being goaded into a sparring match.

In those cases it helps to remember that you are the eyes and ears of your readers. They depend on you to report and write faithfully and honestly about the issues that affect them. If someone in authority is refusing to comment, and you know they have information critical to your readership, then try reassurance. Explain that you understand the concerns. But reiterate the point of your story and why it's important to have that person's perspective to present to your readers.

Or you can politely explain that the story *will* be written—with or without that person's input. "I can try to write a fair story that says you refused to cooperate," you can say, "or I can write a fair story that has your perspective in it." Given the choice, most people opt for the latter.

When a source is being deliberately obtuse and difficult, don't let yourself be pulled into a sparring match. It *is* possible to ask tough questions without being confrontational. For example, by all means ask for a reaction to a negative critique. Just ensure that you aren't using such a question to impart your own opinion.

Be extremely cautious about promising anonymity. Such a guarantee depends on the circumstances, of course, but try to get people to speak on the record. Anonymous sources cast a pall over the reliability of the information in a story. (More on this in Chapter 7.)

Using a tape recorder to ensure accuracy of quotations is usually done as a matter of course. But Muriel Duncan, of *The United Church Observer*, said that during coverage of a particularly sensitive issue she took out her tape recorder to interview a church official, only to watch him take out his. "It didn't seem like a very trustful thing for a Christian to do," she said. "But if that's what it took to get the interview, then that's fine with me. It certainly makes you very careful about what you quote."

Dealing fairly with inexperienced sources

If you're serious about writing meaningful stories—stories that have an impact on people, then you're going to have to seek out sources personally affected by the policies, events and issues you cover. This often means talking to people who don't normally deal with the media. Even though you identify yourself and tell them you want to talk to them about a story you're writing, they still may not get it. They still may not comprehend that what they say to you can wind up in print.

For many, this can be a shocking revelation. It can also be the source of considerable grief for both parties.

There is nothing worse than finishing an interview and then having the person say, "You aren't going to quote me, are you?" Or, just after a source tells you a perfect anecdote or made a revealing admission, he or she turns to you and says, "Of course, you can't print that!"

For David Harris, editor of the Presbyterian Record, attempting to take words off the record when the explicit understanding was that everything was on the record, depends on who's doing the asking. "If I'm talking to a cabinet minister and he says something that is clearly front page news and then wants to back off from what he said, I'm probably not going to let him. He's a politician. He knows who he's talking to and what the parameters of the relationship are. But if I'm talking to someone who misspeaks because they're uptight about talking to me, or if they aren't schooled in how to handle the media, then I might back off. I might stop the interview, explain to them what the process is, and perhaps even ask if they'd like to rephrase what they said."

Though sometimes necessary, ensuring anonymity is the least desirable option.

Rick Hiebert said he consistently finds it hard to get people to go on the record with alternative perspectives on controversial issues. For that reason, he encourages people to write a column. It gives them time to gather their thoughts, to think about how they want to phrase their position.

And you may find you have to perfect your note-taking skills. Ward said he's found that a tape recorder often puts people off. In fact, he's found it makes people so nervous, he tries to work without one. In that case, precise notes are essential.

Asking the right question: The Sawatsky approach

The nub of the interview is *the question*, something that John Sawatsky has perfected to an art. He's an author, journalist and adjunct professor at Carleton University. Sawatsky says that by asking the right question journalists can get almost any information they want.

His interviewing methodology is based on dividing the journalistic process into two steps—input and output. In fact, he often compares the reporter to a fax machine. It has two modes—receiving and sending. But most fax machines can't handle both at the same time.

Receiving and sending, Sawatsky points out, demand opposite skills. And when you put yourself in a "sending" mode when you should be in a "receiving" mode, you miss a lot of information. In an interview situation, this means making yourself a part of the conversation or discussion instead of recognizing your responsibility to obtain information.

Sawatsky said a former prime ministerial press secretary once told him that he had never actually lied to a reporter, but he had "more than once sought refuge in a badly formulated question." Sawatsky now travels the world, teaching journalists how to ask the kinds of questions that will get them the information they need.

In his interviewing workshops he outlines the "seven deadly sins committed by reporters."

1. Making a statement instead of asking a question. Without a question, a source doesn't have to respond. Instead people can effortlessly change the subject and move in any direction they choose.

2. Asking double-barrelled questions. When you ask two questions at the same time, you give sources what Sawatsky calls "an exit ramp." They can answer the question they prefer to answer, not necessarily the one you want them to answer.

3. Overloading your question. This involves broaching too broad a topic. "What do you think of the role of women in the church?" A more specific question would be, "Can you describe your position on the ordination of women?"

4. Inserting remarks into your question. This is the "sin" of being in the sending mode instead of the receiving mode. It involves giving information when you should be getting it, and it runs against the grain of asking a question. It also invites an argument.

5. Using trigger words. They do exactly what the word "trigger" implies—they spark a response, and it's usually a defensive one. This is because trigger words carry a value judgment. In this example, "How many times

did you go on a *junket* to Jerusalem?" *Junket* is a trigger word implying that the trip was merely for personal pleasure but paid for by someone else. Better to ask, "How many times did you travel to Jerusalem?"

6. Exaggerating. If you ask a question that exaggerates an issue or event, then people will respond to the excess in the question, rather than to the nub of the question.

7. Asking a closed question. This kind of question requires only a Yes or No answer. The result is similar to making a statement instead of asking a question; sources can take the interview in the direction they want. It also means a source can avoid having to reveal anything.

Sawatsky suggests operating on three principles when conducting an interview: First, ask open questions—questions that allow a source to explain an aspect of the issue you're exploring. (This is different from an open-ended question, when a source is encouraged to explore a broad topic rather than a specific issue, allowing the source to take the answer in any direction he or she wants.) Such questions, he says, are neither too broad nor close-ended. They deal with the sins of asking closed questions or of asking no question at all.

Second, ask neutral questions. These avoid the sins of interjecting remarks, using trigger words and inserting exaggerations in questions.

Finally, he suggests making your questions "lean." Ask questions that are short and simple. These avoid the sins of double-barrelled or overloaded questions.

People who are media savvy may attempt to entice you into committing one or more of these interviewing sins. For example, they may try to appeal to your ego. "What do *you* think?" they'll ask. Or, "What would *you* do?" Though it's always tempting to impress others with your intellect and experience (especially those in positions of authority), remember that's not why you're there. You're there to get information. You're there on behalf of your readers. Much better to respond to such temptations with, "I'm sure our readers are much more interested in your opinion than mine."

If there's time at the end of an interview, of course there's no harm in having a conversation, but that's another matter.

Sawatsky's guidelines may seem rigid. We've all had the experience of having a comfortable conversation with someone we're interviewing—a "conversation" that involved exchanging thoughts and ideas, while still eliciting worthwhile information.

Of course, humanity is required. Being real. Letting your personality shine through. But the bottom line is, you're doing an interview. You're there for a reason. You're not there to make a friend (although that can, and often does, result). You're not there to impress or to show off how much you know about a subject. (Your chance to shine will come when you sit down to write.) You're there as a professional doing your job. Following Sawatsky's guidelines is a good way to conduct effective interviews.

However, no matter how good guidelines are, that's all they are—guidelines. Beware of following any guideline too rigidly. In fact, there *is* a place for closed questions. There *will* be times when you simply want a straightforward answer to a question. A vote has been cast and you need to know "Who won?" Or you need to know "How much money was raised for the new organ?" Or your readers will want to know "How many people attended mass on Christmas Eve?"

Also, one of the best ways to hook people into reading your article is to begin your story with an anecdote. Often, people don't automatically think to share an anecdote during an interview. Some seem to be under the misapprehension that, because they're speaking to someone from the religious press, pious language is required. Or they might feel the need to talk learnedly, academically. Then perhaps they're nervous and seek comfort in using jargon or language they can hide behind.

What you want, of course, is for them to be themselves, to express themselves naturally—and to tell you anecdotes that illustrate the points they're making. So when people make a statement, don't be afraid to ask for an anecdote to back up that statement.

Also, if sources seem to be deliberately obtuse or hiding inside a cold shell, try asking questions that will draw them out: Where did they come from? What were their parents like? What is a typical day like? Find something you have in common. By exploring that, they might relax and open up.

The adage "Silence is golden" can be applied sparingly in an interview situation. Don't always rush to ask your next question. Sometimes people need extra time to gather their thoughts. A pause can help them do this. A technique that can be used manipulatively (so should be used consciously and carefully in extreme situations) is to maintain silence after an answer. No one likes dead air. People rush to fill it. Often they'll say things they hadn't intended to say, but which may be very revealing.

Oh, one final thing. Save the tough questions for last.

Listening

We were given two ears but only one mouth. This is because God knew that listening was twice as hard as talking.

If one of the first tenets of a good interview is a good question, the second tenet is good listening. There's a reason for the adage, "Listening is hard—really, really hard." But how well you listen can make or break a story. And if you publish something you heard incorrectly or something you heard but didn't verify, then you can break the lives of others.

Think of listening as ministry. People need to tell their stories. They need to be taken seriously. They need to be listened to.

An interview can't be done half-heartedly. You have to *really* listen. You've got to be *alert, present* and *focused*.

Like many of the other skills required to be a good reporter/writer, listening involves a learning process. Why? Most of us have perfected the art of doing a number of things at the same time, with listening being just one of many. But when interviewing, you really need to be there. To be present. To give your full and utter attention to the person you are interviewing. To look him or her in the eye. Not to argue, but to let the person speak. To listen so carefully that you can return to something said earlier in the interview and relate it to the present.

The other important thing to bear in mind is that no matter how much you think you know about a subject—and no matter how much you may have to say about it—the interview is *not* about you. Remind yourself when you go to an interview that when it is over you have to write a story—and you can't quote yourself! You need the source's words in the source's speaking style. If there is ever a situation to put your ego aside, it's when doing an interview. Don't be afraid to sound naïve.

Interviews can be done by phone, in person or via e-mail. Listening has applicability only to the first two, in which case there are advantages and disadvantages to both. The major listening advantage of a face-to-face interview is that you can pay attention to what is said physically, through body language. You're able to look a person in the eye and focus on the answers. And you can use your body language to show that you're listening (looking puzzled, nodding to provide encouragement to continue).

Listening when you're doing a phone interview presents another challenge. In fact, I once heard the phone interview described as "fast food. It serves the purpose, but in a minimal way." You can't see the person, so you can't establish much of a rapport, or read the body language. On the other hand, the person can't read yours, either. So you can put your feet up, eat a muffin, yawn, glance at the morning paper. The problem is, you rapidly lose your ability to listen. You aren't fully concentrating on what's being said.

Bear in mind that the person at the other end of the phone is listening to you. And what that person may be hearing might not be the message you intend to send. You may be asking a perfectly good question, but are expressing through your tone of voice the message, "I'm young and inexperienced and I don't know what I'm doing. Please help me." Conversely, you could be conveying the message, "I'm tired of talking to people like you. I've heard it all before. Be quick so I can get out of here."

Phone and in-person interviews share certain listening features. First, enter into the interview with an open mind. Make sure you are listening for what the person is *really* saying—not for what you hope the person will say. Second, follow up on the answers. Don't just jump to the next question on your list. It can wait.

And even though you're listening carefully, this doesn't mean that you shouldn't interrupt if you don't understand something. Although it's hard to admit ignorance, this is the one situation in which you should never be afraid to acknowledge you need help understanding something. Remember, you have to go back to your desk and make this material accessible. How can you do that if it doesn't make sense to you?

There is no shame in admitting ignorance (unless, of course, you didn't do initial research). And there is certainly nothing wrong in asking people to translate jargon. Sometimes specialists get so caught up in the language of their specialty they forget that outsiders don't speak the same language.

You can't listen well if you aren't well prepared. Leafing through your notebook looking for the next question or rifling through papers trying to find a statistic is unprofessional behaviour.

Finally, all the time you are listening, interpret what is being said; evaluate it; and respond to it. This is called attentive listening. This means asking a question, listening carefully to the answer and then following up with a related question. All the while, however, an attentive listener watches for body cues, reads them and uses them to point in the direction of other questions. Nothing creates a worse impression than asking a question a source has already answered. It conveys inattentiveness, abstraction—even carelessness.

Attentive listeners become adept at catching that relevant quotation at the time it's uttered, picking up that slip of the tongue, that contradiction, those bursts of enthusiasm, signs of tension, what isn't said. Even silence can be revealing.

Group Interviews

You may find yourself in a situation in which you have to interview a number of people at once. This presents its own kind of challenge. For one thing, you may not know everyone. This mean you'll either have to learn names very quickly or ask them to identify themselves when they speak. Depending on the number of people, the former is difficult, and the latter is disruptive. However, you may have no choice but to interrupt. And it certainly beats the alternative, which is attributing a quotation to the wrong person!

To get the most out of such a situation, code your notebook so you can ascertain who said what. And this is a situation in which it's particularly useful to be recording at the same time as taking notes. You may well need to check your tape for backup and confirmation.

Finally, don't let anyone leave without giving you contact information. This should be done as a matter of course with everyone you interview. But it may be especially necessary to contact people for additional comments should your notes or tape prove confusing.

The importance of observation

Once I was interviewing a well-known "personality" who was very experienced in dealing with the media. We were sitting on couches at right angles to each other and sharing a huge, square coffee table. At one point in the interview she responded to a question by reaching for the roasted peanuts on the table and compulsively beginning to gnaw on them. Her voice tone hadn't changed; nor had the expression on her face. But her behaviour signalled to me that we'd touched a nerve.

It wasn't immediately obvious what had spurred that reaction, so I simply drew an asterisk beside the answer she'd given. Then, just as the interview was winding up, I flipped back to it to see what was being discussed and approached that subject from another angle. Indeed, it was a sensitive area, but she responded candidly. In fact, it took us into a completely different avenue of thought and the subsequent profile was not at all what I'd initially envisioned. None of that would have been possible, however, without my picking up on the message her body was inadvertently sending.

Through their bodies, people signal that they're uncomfortable at the line of questioning. They may pull their hair, gnaw on a pencil, shift in their seats or be unable to maintain eye contact. Make a note of that. Then find a way to go back to the question another way—then or later.

Also try to observe the details of a room, the pictures on the wall, the clutter on a desk. All can provide insight into your source's personality or character, or add colour to your story.

Common courtesies

It should go without saying that punctuality is essential. For a variety of reasons, sources often need you to get their perspective across or to tell their side of a story. But approach every interview under the assumption that *you* need *them*. An interview, after all, must be consensual. You can't make anyone talk to you. Why begin on the wrong footing by showing up late? Terrible traffic may be your excuse, but that's almost a given today. So leave early. Don't put yourself in a situation where you keep someone waiting and create a bad impression. (Having said that, my experience is that it's usually sources who run late. Make sure you always carry research material with you so you can put that time to good use.)

Perhaps it's merely conventional wisdom, but the first four minutes of an interview are said to create the tone for the rest of the meeting. So bear in mind that first impressions count. Smile, be polite and set a professional tone right off the bat.

Also, while you are sizing up your source, he or she no doubt is doing the same to you. So dress appropriately. If you're interviewing in an office, don't wear jeans. Conversely, if you're joining the person at a Sunday school picnic, don't wear a formal business suit.

Even though you may be on a tight deadline, don't rush an interview. Let people say what they need to say in the time it takes them to say it. It's not only the respectful thing to do, but often the best material comes during the latter part of an interview when people are feeling comfortable with you and have had some time to gather their thoughts.

And as much as you may be shocked or dismayed by what you hear, don't sit in judgment. Approach every interview with an open mind. And then make every effort to ensure that you are interpreting correctly what the person is saying.

Maintain eye contact. It's a non-verbal form of communication that expresses interest in the other person and helps you hone your attentive listening skills.

Finally, don't ever finish an interview without doing three things. First, get a business card so you are guaranteed the correct spelling of that person's name and position. If that's not appropriate, ask how to spell the name. Don't make any assumptions. (I once assumed that the spelling of a person's last name was "Maddox" simply because I had cousins with that name. At the last moment, however, I thought to ask. And sure enough, the name was spelled "Maddocks.") Also don't assume that spouses share the same last name or that their children carry their father's name. Ask for full names and the correct spelling of those names.

Second, don't leave an interview without asking whether the person can recommend anyone else for you speak to about this issue or suggest further reading material. Then ask if you've covered all the turf or whether the person thinks there's something else worth exploring. Those questions can be gold mines!

And finally, thank the person. This person has given you time and perhaps even has put himself or herself on the line. Remember, too, this may not be the end of the relationship. You may need to return to this source for this or another story. Leave a good impression. Leave the impression the person has been dealing with a pro!

After the interview

You'll be doing yourself a great favour if you take the time, after an interview, to transcribe your notes immediately. Transcribing tapes is a long and arduous process. Instead, you might want to fast forward to a part of the tape where you know you'll find a good quotation. (You do this by setting your tape recorder counter at 0 when the interview begins, and then periodically adding the counter reading as you take notes.)

This is also a good time to either jot down what you observed or to elaborate on your observations. Do it while everything is still fresh in your memory. You may think you'll never forget that a purple copy of the 1903 Book of Common Prayer (Edward VII) was lying open on a linen-covered drop-leaf table. But it's amazing how quickly those details disappear. Add the non-verbal observations—facial expressions, body language, what the person was wearing.

Once you've deciphered your shorthand, arrange your notes in order of importance. To save time, I often highlighted the themes and/or quotations I thought I'd probably use. It's also important to note the statements or statistics you'll need to verify with other sources. Compile a list of what to verify and with whom (or where).

Never be afraid to call sources back to check quotations or information for accuracy. Don't assume you're being a nuisance. Also don't assume they'll think less of you because you didn't get everything straight the first time round. Most people would much prefer to invest the time to help you get everything right than to deal with the fallout from omissions or inaccuracies. And your insistence on precision and accuracy will also ensure that they view you as a pro.

If you made a commitment during the interview, make sure you keep it. For example, you might have said that the article will appear in the next edition. But things happen, line-ups change. If it's not going to appear then, let the person know immediately (friends and family have probably been told to be on the lookout for it). And if you said it would be a feature story but now it'll wind up as a sidebar, also let the person know that in advance.

Finally, if you promised to send a copy of the published article, make a note to yourself to do so—and follow through.

However, if the person asked to see a copy of the article *before* it is printed, then that's a promise you should never have made in the first place. (This issue will be fully explored in Chapter 7.)

Writing Journalistically

Put it before them briefly, so they will read it, clearly so they will appreciate it, picturesquely so they will remember it, and above all, accurately, so they will be guided by its light.

– *Joseph Pulitzer (1847–1911),*
U.S. newspaper publisher

A number of years ago, David Harris, then editor of the *Anglican Journal,* assigned a reporter to write about the Canadian Council of Churches' decision to ask Canadian tourists to boycott Florida. The Council had suggested that if any members of their congregations were thinking of taking a holiday in the sun, they try Cuba instead of Florida.

"This was not fuelled by a pro-Castro sentiment, but by an anti-U.S. sentiment," said Harris. (Many church people felt the U.S. was punishing Cuba economically, thereby contributing to suffering.) "We reported [the tourism suggestion], and [council members] were pleased. But reaction was swift. People thought it was a crock. Later we followed up on this story by looking at tourism figures in Florida and Cuba. What we found was that the boycott was a total flop. More people visited Florida than ever before."

This finding was then reported on the front page of the paper—a situation that upset a number of church officials. Harris was quietly taken aside and told he should have "played" the story differently. "But I said, 'If this boycott had been a success, would you have expected it to be covered on the front page?'" said Harris. "While the answer, of course, was 'Yes', they still felt I was being 'disloyal' to give the follow-up story such prominence."

No doubt every editor working for a religious publication has struggled with this kind of situation. Look at an event, an issue, dispassionately, and it's clear there is a legitimate news story. However, look at the same material through the lens of a church official or a loyal reader who wants to protect the church or denomination, and it takes on a completely different colour. "We get criticism from people who think we should only show the good face of Catholicism to the world," said Joe Sinasac, editor of *The Catholic Register*. "I can see their point insofar as there are good things happening and no one knows about them. Our role is to print that. But there are also many debates taking place—the Catholic church is a big community with a lot of different people—and we try to be a forum for those debates. We try to shed light on issues.

"In our reporting," he added, "we try to impart what people need to know. And sometimes that involves political controversies."

Part of the problem for the religious press is that many of the lay readership, as well as many church officials, don't have any idea what news is. Nor do they understand what role their publication should play in reporting it. This puts editors, and often writers, in the position of not only covering the news, but of trying to educate their readership about *why* something is newsworthy.

There are probably as many definitions of "news" as there are publications. There's "true, timely and in the public interest." There's "timely, important and interesting." There's "anything that helps people prepare for change." And from *The Canadian Reporter*, comes my favourite, "significant, interesting and new," or SIN.

Regardless of the definition, a judgment call has to be made before something appears as a news story. On what basis is that decision made? A priority consideration should be the readership. Who reads your publication? What are they interested in? What do they need to know?

To help make a judgment call, editors and reporters rely on something called "news values." It isn't that they have a list of "news values" that they tick off each time something happens and then tally up to determine whether the total justifies writing a story. But editors and writers *do* always approach potential stories with an awareness of what constitutes news.

You'll need to choose your stories on the basis of the news values most relevant to your readership and to your publication. But here are the news values Melvin Mencher, a former journalism professor at Columbia University, thinks professionals should consider when making a judgment call.

News values

Timeliness. Something happens—an event, an issue. The newness of it makes it newsworthy.

Impact. This is a news value people often find difficult to understand. Why pay so much attention to what's happening in a church in Toronto when something similar is happening in my church in the rural community of...(you fill in the blank). The reality is that something that affects a lot of people is usually going to get more copy—and be more prominently displayed—than a story affecting only a handful.

Prominence. The better known the people or institution, the more news coverage a story that involves them will probably get.

Proximity. The closer an event is to people, either geographically or emotionally, the more interest they will have in reading about it.

Conflict. Conflict occurs at a variety of levels—conflict between countries, between ideologies, between institutions, between people. But there are also the kinds of conflicts that people confront in their daily lives. The struggle to find God in the face of tragedy. The effort to overcome an addiction. This is the "human drama" that often makes the story interesting to the rest of us.

Currency. This captures the sense of an idea whose time has come. Because of the tenor of the times or a set of circumstances coming together, something is now being discussed and debated. In other words, it is relevant. It has "currency."

Necessity. This relates to information a writer or editor has discovered and which, in that person's opinion, should be disclosed to the readership.

There's another news value that Lloyd Mackey, editorial director of *ChristianCurrent*, Ottawa edition, often considers. He calls it "conciliation." By this he means using his stories to reach out to disparate parts of the Christian community, looking for ways to come together, to be reconciled. Too often he's seen the "conflict" news value applied inappropriately.

For example, Mackey said that once, when he was writing for *Western Report* magazine in Edmonton, the publisher, Ted Byfield, called him over to his computer. Mackey had filed a story about research being done on narwhals in the Arctic in light of oil exploration in the area. Mackey gave it the headline: "Oil and Whales." Byfield, however, deleted the "and" and substituted "vs." to make the headline read "Oil vs. Whales."

Mackey said Byfield explained the change on the grounds

that every story needs conflict. Otherwise, he told him, people won't be interested.

"But conflict wasn't the point of that story," said Mackey. "Being able to report on and write about conflict is important in journalism. But there are also opportunities for Christians to overlay the conciliation concept."

Mackey compares the concept of conciliation to a transparency—the clear sheet of material you can write on and lay over documents. Transparencies allow other elements to be displayed in relation to what already exists. "You don't eliminate conflict if it exists," said Mackey, "but you illuminate other elements. In some cases, doing that will dissolve the conflict because there is an element of conflict resolution in the conciliation. But in some cases, of course, the conflict won't go away. Then it's important to be realistic. Not to sugarcoat the situation."

Applying the principle of conciliation, Mackey said, "helps different parts of the community see others in a way that briefly introduces them to each other." It's a way, he said, of being thought provoking without being inflammatory. In fact, it might involve backing off a story if the potential for misunderstanding among the readership exists. He said that applying the value of conciliation to news might mean looking for ways to communicate a story so that misunderstandings will be minimized. (A potential risk in this approach could lie in underestimating the ability of your readers to come to their own conclusions about the positions people take—provided, of course, that they've been given all the facts.)

Whatever your "news values," when you apply your creative instincts as well as your powers of critical thinking to evaluate the significance of issues and events, then you're using "news judgment." Editors follow the same kind of criteria to determine the length of a story and its placement.

One of the most common criticisms relayed to writers and editors—in both the secular and religious press—is that they concentrate too much on the bad news. But if those same people regularly opened up their daily paper or their monthly Christian magazines only to find such headlines as "10,000 planes land safely at the Toronto airport today" or "No Canadian churches demolished by fire this month," they'd soon realize why news really is about more than the commonplace, the ordinary or the "good."

Having said that, "good" doesn't have to mean mundane. There are certainly good-news stories that are anything but pedestrian. The point is not that good news is boring, but that it generally doesn't embrace the whole truth about an event or an issue. It's your job to report responsibly—warts and all!

Ultimately there's no "right" way to make a judgment call on what should be a news story or on how prominently it should be displayed. Following the SIN rule (significant, interesting, new) is a good guide, however. Then see how the news values of your publication stack up against SIN. However resolved you may be in taking this course of action, the reality is that news judgments aren't made in isolation. Sometimes you may make a decision not to run with a story, only to find that you have to play catch-up because the mainstream press is covering the story and you need to provide another perspective.

You might decide that a story should be covered but then don't have the resources to do so. In that case you will have to decide whether to pick up the story off the wire and find local sources to interview and insert into the story (to provide your own "spin," or "take" on it).

Finally, take the time after you've made a judgment call to honestly assess the basis on which you made your decision. Did you make the decision for the right reasons (by following your news values)? Or did you decide to take the route of least resistance (ruffling no feathers) that, in the process, does a disservice to your readers?

Making a judgment call on what is news is a big responsibility. Often you have to make that decision on the run, in the midst of an event, or even in the middle of interviewing someone. The best advice I can offer is that the more you know about your readership, as well as the larger world in which they find themselves, the better prepared you'll be to make a judgment call you can feel good about.

Just as important, it'll be one that you'll be able to stand by should you face criticism.

Basic elements of news

If you've decided that a story should be written because it contains essential news values, then it should contain certain basic elements. It helps to remember them by bearing in mind that you're the surrogate for your readers—their eyes and ears. You aren't writing about your perspective on an issue or an event. In fact, you should consciously try to set that aside and approach every story with as open a mind as possible.

Try to ensure that every question your readers might want, or need, to be answered is addressed. This means, first and foremost, answering the *five Ws and H* (who, what, when, where, why and how). In addition, readers might well add, *So what?* So address it. Help them to understand why a story matters, how it is connected to their lives, and whether it relates to a larger theme or issue.

A news story should also include a sense of *time*. Readers need to be oriented. They need to know when an event occurred, its historical context or when it is expected to occur.

News usually also has a sense of *drama*. This is something that people who are in the news often get most disgruntled about. They'd prefer to have an event or issue—and certainly their role in it—downplayed. But news is action. It's people

81

doing things, being involved with each other and often being in conflict with each other.

In addition, news should have both a sense of *place* and a sense of *people*. This means actually taking your readers to where the action is. It means not simply giving them the names and titles of people, but, if possible and appropriate, providing telling details that make those people come alive.

It means getting more than one perspective on any story. Rewriting a press release by talking only to official spokespeople is one way to write a news story. But it won't be a very good one. Seek out sources who can provide other perspectives—especially those who might be most intimately affected by an issue. This helps provide *fairness and balance* and originality.

Accuracy and precision are also essential. Names must be correctly spelled, details described accurately, and the stance that people take on an issue must be precisely presented—and, most definitely, must not be taken out of context.

Then there are *attribution and verification*. Statements must be attributed to the sources who made them, and facts must be verified, or checked out.

Finally, there is *diversity*. Diversity of opinion, as mentioned, but also, diversity of sources in terms of age, gender and race. In other words, strive to interview people who reflect the actual demographics of your church or denomination, as well as the demographics of those affected by the story.

Where does news come from?

News comes from a variety of places—from press releases, news conferences, annual general assemblies, retreats, official records and what you see or hear in the course of your reporting. A lot of news flows from events and from the decisions and actions made by people in power. But news also comes from those who are not functionaries but whose stories matter.

Types of stories

The kind of story you'll write will depend very much upon the nature of the event or issue. It will also depend upon your branch of journalism—reporting or commentary. Reporting is giving an account of an event after researching and investigating it. Commenting is critiquing something that is in the news. Although often it's simply a "rant," commentary (in the form of column writing or editorial writing) should be informed opinion or critical analysis.

What follows is a brief outline of the variety and scope of journalistic writing.

Stories based on reporting

NEWS STORIES

News stories can be split into two types: hard news and soft news. Both should express their message clearly and succinctly. This means writing short sentences in everyday language. It also means having an obvious focus, or theme, and a coherent structure.

Tell readers what happened, why it's important, and what might happen next.

Hard news refers to event-based stories—such as a meeting of bishops or a fatal bus accident carrying children to Sunday school. It also refers to depth coverage—to stories that explore issues.

Here's an example of a hard news story that ran in *Canada Lutheran*, the January–February 2003 edition.

In a landmark judgement, the Supreme Court of Canada has ruled against allowing Harvard University a patent on a mouse that has been genetically modified for medical research. The ruling, which ends a 17-year legal battle, is a victory for churches that had argued that patenting the mouse would mean turning living beings into intellectual property.

Soft news is much more difficult to define. Often it involves stories that aren't pegged to a specific event. In fact, often they're stories involving people or things that people *want* to know about, as opposed to stories about people or things that they *should* know about. There is usually a discretionary quality about soft news stories. It's safe to say that soft news stories are usually human interest stories.

Assessing whether the story has a sense of immediacy is one way of determining which category it would fall into. If you think your readers would not be ill-served to have it sit on the back burner until you have the space to run it, then it is probably soft news.

Here's a story that could be pegged as soft news. Entitled "Family histories in a shoebox," it ran in the December 2002 issue of the *Anglican Journal*. Written by Leanne Larmondin (now the acting editor), the story describes the attempt to get people who are dying of AIDS in South Africa to put memories of their life into a box for their children.

> I wonder who would be interested in this set of silverware," Mum said, polishing a fork before a recent family dinner. Dad was elsewhere in the house trying to load up my eldest brother with some of his future inheritance....
>
> It seems both my parents are thinking ahead about what they would like to pass along when they, well, pass along.
>
> My family's heirlooms are scattered throughout the family house: odd bits of furniture, china, untouchable crystal, the Bible with our modest genealogy inside. There are albums of photographs from my mother's and even my grandfather's youth. Generally, I know the provenance of these items, their stories.

• • •

I didn't meet the man in the Tumelong AIDS hospice, but I was honoured and also embarrassed to get a glimpse into life. I remember thinking, "This is what grace is all about." His life was being documented in a memory box. Some of his memories were carefully noted in a small booklet, loose sheets of paper, tied with cheerful little bows of yarn....

Regardless of whether you're writing a hard news story or soft news story, you should meet certain minimum standards. First, state your focus, or theme, clearly and keep on track. Second, let your readers know whether what you're writing about will have any consequences for them. People care about how events or policy decisions will affect their lives. So tell them.

Third, use anecdotes and quotations to illustrate points you're making. Don't use them to decorate your story. If they aren't relevant to your story, then leave them out.

Fourth, always strive to provide insight. This sometimes means asking Why? of a lot of people. A good rule of thumb is to have at least three sources in a news story.

ANALYTICAL STORIES

"In-depth" or "interpretive" is another way to describe analytical stories. Carleton journalism professor David Tait said analytical reporters don't just cover events; they spot trends, emerging issues and promising breakthroughs. In addition, he said, they probe "deeply enough into them to be able to tell the community how they came about, what they mean, and what lies ahead."

Analytical stories aren't necessarily long, although they do run longer than news stories. (In a magazine they can run to 3,000 words.) They should contain action and description, details and numbers (if applicable), and a range of sources (depending on the length of the story, between six and 10). The sources should provide balance—in other words, presenting perspectives from all sides of an issue. And those sources should be quoted.

Ultimately, of course, analytical stories must deliver on their promise—they must provide analysis. You should tell readers how something came about, what an event means or what could lie ahead.

Carleton journalism professor Roger Bird said the number one rule for anyone attempting to write analytical stories is, "You've got to know your area." This means knowing who to talk to in the community, in officialdom (church leaders, government officials, academics and other specialists) and what groups or organizations are affected by your subject as well as having a broad and comprehensive understanding of your topic.

FEATURE STORIES

More like a non-fiction short story, a good feature should be informative, entertaining, descriptive and peppered with people. It should also be original, both in the way in which it's written and in its approach to the subject.

Why worry about originality if you've got an interesting subject? Well, a feature is considerably longer than a news story, meaning you're asking readers to devote a chunk of time they may not necessarily think they have to give. But if you want them to take this journey with you, then you must provide an unforgettable experience.

Gail Reid, managing editor of *Faith Today*, said she frequently gets features that consist of virtually nothing but quotations strung together. "Also," she added, "I find that writers tend to think that because a feature is longer [than a news story], they can go on and on and on. Instead, what they should be doing is aiming for simple language and tight writing."

News stories are usually written so that people can scan the first few paragraphs of a story and get the gist of it. However, a feature story is more fluid in structure and must be read from beginning to end to make sense. (This presents a challenge for editors because unlike a conventional news story, they can't cut for length by trimming from the end. Careful cutting throughout the text is required.)

Regardless of whether a story is news, analysis or a feature, however, it must meet professional standards. Information should be verified, quotations must be accurate and the story should be fair and balanced, based on a diversity of sources.

In addition, it should conform to the style standards set by the publication. Many follow Canadian Press (CP) style guidelines with regard to punctuation, capitalization, abbreviation, titles and spelling.

Just because a story is a feature, however, doesn't mean that writers and editors won't have to face disgruntled readers—readers who don't understand the purpose of a story. People who instinctively want their view of the world confirmed in their publication. When confronted with anything to the contrary, they raise a hue and cry.

When Marianne Meed Ward was managing editor of *Faith Today*, for example, her team worked on a cover story on sexuality. "It was 15 pages long and one and a half pages were devoted to homosexuality," she said. "Within that page and a half, someone who'd written on homosexual relations in the '60s was quoted. His book had been reprinted and he'd added a chapter to it. In it, he said he was now wondering if a committed monogamous homosexual relationship, although less than God's ideal, was better than promiscuous relationships."

"There was a huge outcry," said Meed Ward. "It was unbelievable. We were even targeted by a particular group and picketed. It astonished me. It's not as if we were introducing theology outside the evangelical fold. But the view in many Christian circles was that publication was equal to condoning. My reaction was, 'Don't you people want to know about what's going on? Don't you want to understand issues? Don't you want to know what people think?'"

Though Meed Ward has done a lot of writing for the secular press, she said she's never encountered that kind of thinking there. "They don't labour under the idea that just because you publish something, you agree with it. As a result, you see more diversity."

Though the upheaval caused by the article was difficult to deal with, at another level Meed Ward welcomed it. "It was my chance to give people a new understanding of the role of the press," she said. "I relished the challenge."

Types of feature stories

There are various types of feature stories: human interest, profiles and those based on hard news. Though a feature can be about almost anything, it usually revolves around an unusual person, place, activity or issue. And though not every feature will have universal appeal, the best will make a statement that is meaningful to the human condition.

HUMAN INTEREST

A human interest story means exactly what it says: it's about whatever interests people. A good guide as to what qualifies is this: If something interests you, the writer, or your editor, then it will probably also pique the interest of a substantial number of readers.

Human interest stories can be about people or things, but people stories are generally far more interesting and have wider readership appeal than stories about things. They also invite description in a way that news stories don't. (Because news stories are shorter and have a sense of urgency, any description must be essential to the focus.) Description is essential in feature writing because it evokes imagery and helps transport readers to the person or place being described.

In the September–October 2002 edition of *Faith Today*, for example, N.J. Lindquist wrote a cover story entitled, "Why we're reading Christian fiction."

> A woman in your church has a bruise on her cheek. She says she tripped, but you have your own suspicions. You could: mind your own business; offer advice over a cup of coffee; buy her a book on relationships; lend her your copy of *Sadie's Song*, a suspense novel that tells the story of a Christian woman who comes to realize she is being abused by her husband, a deacon.

> Deborah Gyapong of Ottawa says she'd give the novel because it meets an abused person's need "to see a spark of recognition, compassion and understanding from a Christian standpoint."...

> What's going on...is not new, but it is increasing: more and more people are reading novels by Christian authors. Christian fiction is in a growth phase like the one Christian music was in 10 years ago. Fiction sales are now 15 percent of the Christian book market for adults, compared to a mere 4.3 percent in 1985....

PROFILE

A profile gives readers the opportunity to gain insight into someone's life—into how the person looks, sounds, behaves and thinks. But a profile is only as effective as your ability to make that person come alive. Often a single, well-chosen word can breathe life into someone. Or you might find a detail, a gesture, a snapshot view of the person's study or reading material that connects the subject to your readers.

Aim to provide details that convey a sense of intimacy without a corresponding sense of invasion.

Practically anyone or anything can be profiled. Of course, profiles are usually written about people, with their cooperation. You choose someone of interest, ask for an interview, and then research and interview people who know them. Although groups and institutions can be profiled, this is less common. Yet that's exactly what Donna Sinclair did in the June 2002 edition of *The United Church Observer*. She profiled the work being done by parish nurses, work that reclaims "the link between religion and medicine."

As Winnipeg parish nurse Angela Cook came down the hospital corridor, she could hear a woman moaning. She soon found out it was the 86-year-old she was coming to visit. The woman was sitting in the dusk, in a geriatric chair, wearing a hospital gown open at the back. She was cold. Her swollen feet had slipped off the footrests, which had pressed an indentation into one foot.

"I'm from the church," said Cook, who is on staff at Sturgeon Creek United. She got her a glass of water and a warm blanket, put socks on her feet and got them elevated, all the time repeating, "I'm from the church." The woman stopped moaning and they talked about childhood on the farm and walking to school. Had she gone to Sunday school, Cook asked, did she ever think about God? The woman looked up. 'Why would I think about God?' she said clearly. 'He hates me.' She told the parish nurse she'd had an affair long ago, and had been shunned ever after by her own family and her husband's family. "We had a chat about God's love," says Cook quietly, "and I said a prayer for God's forgiveness." The next time Cook visited, the nurses wondered what Cook had done; the elderly woman was now sleeping so well....

FIRST-PERSON FEATURES

Most feature stories are written in the third person. However, sometimes, something so dramatic happens to the writer, it begs to be told in the first person.

For example, Michael McAteer wrote in the January–February 2003 edition of *Canada Lutheran* about a fact-finding trip he took to the Middle East. It was entitled "Report from East Jerusalem."

> East Jerusalem—It's my last day in the so-called Holy Land and I'm standing in one of the Old City's narrow streets watching four armed young Israeli soldiers search and interrogate three young Palestinians.
>
> One of the soldiers turns and glares at me. "Yes?" he barks, his tone hostile, his body language menacing. I tell him I'm just standing, watching. 'Well, can I help you?' he asks curtly.
>
> No, I tell him, I'm just standing, watching. "Well, move," he says.
>
> Anger smothers fear and I stand my ground. For a few tense moments our eyes lock before he turns away. The Palestinians are released and I move on.
>
> For the past seven days I've travelled through the West Bank and the Gaza strip—Israel's occupied territories—on a Lutheran World Federation-sponsored field trip. And I'm consumed by anger at what I've seen and experienced. I had read reports of human rights abuses, of collective punishment, of the daily harassment and intimidation of the occupied by the occupiers. But nothing prepared me for the on-the-ground experience....

A first-person account might describe surviving a plane crash, a nearly fatal car accident with a drunk driver or perhaps a mountain-climbing experience. However, first-person writing should be reserved for the dramatic, the intimately personal, or perhaps the specialist. Readers aren't necessarily as interested in reading about "me, myself and I" as we think they are!

A NEWS FEATURE

When something is happening in the news, and you know it deserves an in-depth treatment, then writing a feature story about it is as good as it gets. It's a way of providing readers with in-depth treatment of a complicated idea or situation. Good quotations and a writing style and tone that are in sync with the subject matter are essential.

For example, in the December 8, 2002 edition of *The Catholic Register*, Michael Swan wrote a feature on the impact that provincial funding cuts are having on Ontario's Catholic school system. It was entitled "The business of education: Funding cuts have created a new underclass in our schools."

> Ontario's Catholic students finally have the same funding as their public school counterparts, but parents are now shelling out after-tax dollars just to ensure their children will have a chance at post-secondary education and a career. Massive underfunding has turned the dream of funding equity into a nightmare of educational inequality, according to Catholic educators.
>
> "At first blush the equity in education concept—from the point of view of Ontario Catholic education—was understood to mean that publicly supported Catholic schools would finally be funded at the same, traditionally higher level, as public schools," said Holy Cross Father Jim Mulligan.... "But it soon became very clear—very soon in the Harris government—that traditional public school funding would not be the norm. Instead, public school budgets would be pared toward traditionally lower Catholic school funding levels." ...

A NEWS SERIES

When an issue can't be adequately covered in one story, you might want to think about writing a series. This is a way of making a complex issue accessible by keeping one central focus, while continuing to explore secondary issues. Think of a series as akin to peeling back the petals to get to the heart of an artichoke. All the petals are integral to the whole and have something to contribute. But they invariably lead to the heart.

Most series run between three and five parts. Why? It's hard to devote more space when other, equally valid stories, are competing for space. And reader fatigue needs to be considered. Most people don't want to read more than three to five stories about an issue.

Having said that, there's always an exception. The 10-part *Sins of the Fathers* series that was described earlier was so compelling and comprehensive that it ran in its own special section.

Not necessarily news nor feature

OBITUARIES

There will be times when you'll need or want to write an obituary of someone who's meant a lot to your faith community or to you personally. Though one of the themes of this book is the need to write accurately and sensitively, perhaps there is no single time at which those characteristics are more sacrosanct than when you write an obituary.

In most cases an obituary will be the last words ever written about someone. They will be particularly meaningful to that person's loved ones. And, of course, not only will the loved ones be quick to notice any errors or omissions, but they could feel betrayed, even have the reputation of their family marred, by inaccuracies.

Some details are essential: name, age, occupation and address. Time, place and cause of death should also be included as well as the names of survivors and burial plans. But what will remain imprinted in the memory of readers are the details that encapsulate that person's qualities and point to the things the person was involved with or contributed to.

Work hard to find what that person did that best reflected who he or she was. Talk to relatives, friends, co-workers, members of the same congregation. Ask for anecdotes. If he or she was a public figure "check the clips" or look up the person in the *Who's Who in Canada*.

Though many writers tend to view the writing of obits as a sign that, professionally, they've come to "the end of the road," some of the finest writing should be found there. Obituaries provide the opportunity to weave together anecdotes, description, facts, the way that person searched for meaning and how the person affected the lives of others. They're also a way of incorporating social history because they not only tell readers something about the deceased, they can also convey something about the times in which they lived.

Here's the intro to an obituary with the headline "Willard Oxtoby 1933–2003: Scholar was 'hooked' on religion." It was written by Ron Csillag and ran in the March 31, 2003 edition of *The Globe and Mail*.

Like members of the clergy and their early epiphanies, scholars of religion can often pinpoint the instant they decided to pursue their calling.

For Willard Oxtoby, one of the world's foremost students of comparative religion and founding director of the University of Toronto's Centre for Religious Studies, a defining moment came at the tender age of five, when his father, a teacher of Old Testament at a Presbyterian seminary, taught his son to memorize the 23rd psalm, in Hebrew. One night, while an advanced Hebrew class met at the Oxtoby home, young Willard was summoned, in his pyjamas, to recite the psalm.

"See?" his father told the class. "Even a kid can do Hebrew, so get on with it." . . .

Commentary

It wasn't that long ago that journalism and opinion were synonymous. But in the 19th century, news and opinion separated. The separation was needed so readers could develop a trust in their news coverage. They needed to know that when they read the news, they weren't being given an account of an event or issue from an interested party. They needed to know that a conscientious effort had been made by trained professionals to present a fair and balanced account.

When readers turned to commentary, however, it was equally important that they found an opinion on the events or issues of the day. Today commentary has evolved into editorials and columns. Editorials present the formal policies and beliefs of a publication. Columnists, however, present their personal "take" on events or issues.

Writing commentary can be exhilarating and intellectually stimulating. It can also be terrifying. Commentary is opinion, and virtually everyone has an opinion about something. Often people become so mired in their own way of looking at things that they don't want to hear anyone else's. Commentary is inherently controversial. Be prepared for reaction, even vituperation.

When people react negatively to an opinion piece, it may not necessarily be because they've already made up their minds and are closed to an opposing perspective. It may be that the opinion wasn't based on adequate research or thought. Perhaps the editorial writer or columnist took the cheap route of a knee-jerk reaction or indulged in a predictable rant. In that case, a negative response is understandable. Readers expect more—and should be given it. Commentators are not exempt from accountability. They must justify their positions with proper research and supporting evidence.

Opinion pieces can be found in editorials, columns and letters to the editor. I love reading letters to the editor. They provide a genuine insight into the readership of a publication as well as a snapshot of diversity of thought. In this next section we'll examine column writing and editorials in particular.

EDITORIAL WRITING

There is no magic formula for writing editorials. They vary widely—as they should—depending on the writing style of the editorial writers and the publications for which they write. But an editorial that simply restates an issue and then tacks on a few lines of criticism at the end is not doing the work of an editorial.

A good editorial should be constructed carefully, so the writer can explain, interpret and appraise an event or issue. It should challenge readers to further thought and debate. And it goes without saying that an editorial is always about something timely.

Editorial writers can make their point through humour, a very effective and humane alternative to ridicule. Badly written humour, however, should be avoided. Humorous editorials are not common. Instead, most editorial writers provide a serious interpretation and analysis of an issue or event. They set the scene by briefly describing the issue at hand, provide interpretation and analysis, and then, if applicable, suggest a course of action.

Underlying all of is this a sound knowledge base. Good editorial writers must be trained thinkers. They should have specialized knowledge in a wide variety of fields. But, given that they can't be knowledgeable in everything, they must be conscientious and thorough researchers. Finally, they must be able to use English effectively and write compellingly.

Editorials should be relatively short; they seldom run more than 1,000 words. For example, a terrific editorial ran in the November 12, 2002 issue of *Christian Week*. Entitled "Fissures in the fellowship," it deals with a dispute occurring in the Fellowship of Evangelical Baptist Churches in Canada over the role of women in church leadership. Written by Doug Koop, it was a signed editorial.

Koop noted the ways in which the Fellowship attempts to uphold "right" doctrine, and he commended the effort. But he questioned whether delivering "right" doctrine and defining differences is as important as reaching out to others in Christian love. Here is a lengthy excerpt.

> ...The impulse to be right militates against the mandate to be missional; the quality of comfortable closeness puts human limits on the wideness of God's mercy. An interpretation of Paul's teaching on women may be rigorously upheld; Christ's words about unity sadly neglected. The Fellowship, for example, cannot quite bring itself to seek full membership in the Evangelical Fellowship of Canada.
>
> In his observations of cultures, eminent Bible translator Eugene Nida has noted that "when people become insecure and uncertain under the impact of pluralism, they normally retreat to a conservative position and demand greater and greater conformity by all those whom they regard as belonging to the same in-group."
>
> We might call it "circling the wagons," assuming a defensive position that fails to communicate a confident gospel message of good news for all. "I do think we can hold the Fellowship together, but only if we can convince the egalitarians to graciously leave. Not expel them, but ask them to see the wisdom and rightness of leaving," says

a leading proponent of the push within the Fellowship for doctrinal clarity and purity.

The Word of God to His people when they were returning to the promised land after a period of captivity is instructive to devout Christians eager to proclaim a message of truth in Canada today, helpful to a minority with a story to tell in the midst of [a] largely indifferent general population. "Enlarge the site of your tent, and let the curtains of your habitations be stretched out; do not hold back; lengthen your cords and strengthen your stakes" (Isaiah 54:2).

When "strengthening your stakes" means faithfully following the dictates of Scripture, be steadfast. But don't close the tent curtains in the process. Fellowship worthy to claim the name of Jesus is embracing, not confining. "Lengthen your cords." Christian mission is difficult in a gated community.

Koop's editorial did what it should have: it explored the issue and eloquently and articulately stated a position. As a result, the editorial caused a furor. "But we try to foster dialogue," he said. "That ticks people off, but we have both [sides of an issue] at home within our papers. People had their say in return. We got lots of letters to the editor, and the president of the Fellowship Baptists wrote a guest column in response."

In other words, the editorial did exactly what it was supposed to do. It got people thinking, responding, debating and perhaps even moving a step closer to resolving an important issue.

COLUMN WRITING

A column is closely related to an editorial, but it differs in a couple of significant ways. First, it's a reflection of the personal views of the writer only—not the publication as a whole. Second, it can embody significantly different writing styles.

Some columnists write in the first person. (Editorials normally are not signed.) And because columns are personal, the personality of the writer should shine through. But all columnists *should* speak from an informed position. They should do the hard work of researching a topic. Then they should do the even harder work of trying to figure out what the issue means to them.

Columnists should also remember that they write from a position of power. With that power comes a particular responsibility to be accountable. Being a columnist is not a license to pursue personal vendettas.

Marianne Meed Ward writes a column for both the mainstream press (the *Toronto Sun*) and the religious press (*ChristianWeek*). She noticed that though she might write on the same issue for both publications, she writes them the two columns quite differently. "I'm often more critical of the Christian community in *ChristianWeek*," she said, "and I wondered why. Then I figured it's like a family. When you get together there are no holds barred. But when the neighbours come over you're more circumspect. When we're talking to ourselves, we should be able to critique ourselves."

Meed Ward said readers can count on an opinion from her, an opinion that is grounded in her faith. What they can't count on, however, is dogma. "In fact, you could say that the only thing I'm dogmatic about is that we don't know everything. I wouldn't say, 'This is the only position a person of faith can take on an issue,' because I don't know the mind of God. I *can* say that, on my interpretation of scripture and within the ethics of Christianity, I look at every issue I tackle in faith and with love and redemption as the framework."

Finally, she said that if there's any side she comes down

on, it's the one that asks, "Can we help people? Or are we erecting barriers in an attempt to solve a problem? Are our rules more important than the spirit that lay behind them?"

Focus

Every story (whether it's news or a feature) and every commentary (whether it's personal opinion or an editorial) needs a focus. Other words refer to the focus, such as the theme, the core, the angle or the central idea. Focus is a good word, though, as it conjures images of a camera. When you focus on something you make that thing stand out; you sharpen it.

It might help if you think of writing out your focus as a focus statement. You'll need a subject, an active verb and the word "because." Someone is doing something to someone for a reason. Here's a hypothetical focus statement: Michelle Tompkins is convinced the Prayer Line will grow with the help of enthusiastic church members because an expanded service will better meet the needs of more people.

As straightforward as the word "focus" may sound, however, beginning writers can get confused. Perhaps your editor assigned you a topic. That's fine—but don't be misled into thinking that your topic is your focus. They are two completely different things. When you get a topic, you begin by researching it. Then you'll find your focus. (Or, your editor might give you a focus. Even better, as this economizes the research process. But don't be so committed to that focus that you can't change it if research points you in another direction.)

Without a focus, a story not only flounders and dies, but it can take its author with it. This is not an exaggeration. If you become known as someone who can't focus your stories, then your writing career will be short-lived. No one wants to read a story that has clearly been given little or no thought.

No one wants to wade through copy that doesn't seem to have a point.

Thinking is the first step in finding your focus. Thinking about the research you've done. Thinking about its implications. Thinking about where it leads you. In fact, thinking is what allows you to transform the information you've gathered into knowledge. And how do you do that thinking? Well, applying your powers of critical thinking is one obvious step. But there are others. You might talk your story over with your editor or with a friend. Tell the person what you've learned. Your focus, or theme, will often appear as you attempt to answer the question, So what? or as you struggle to find the significant, the profound.

You might also try closing your notebooks and beginning to write without any research materials at hand. What comes to the surface? What emerges as significant? Use this process as a way of interviewing yourself. If you did solid research, then you're now something of an expert on the subject. So, what's the story? What did you learn? If you tried to sum everything up in one sentence, one paragraph, what would it be? What's the focus?

Or write a theme paragraph—one that you'd write for readers to tell them what this story is about. (This is also known as a "nut graf.") In fact, you might try writing a focus statement and attaching it to your computer or pinning it on a bulletin board beside your desk. Refer to it as you organize your material and write. It'll help remind you to stay on track.

You may feel you're under a tight deadline and can't afford the exploration time. But it's much better to spend time finding and sharpening your focus than facing a frustrated or disappointed editor and then having to plough your way through a lengthy rewrite process.

Patria Rivera, editor of the magazine *Catholic Missions in*

Canada (formerly *Mission Canada*), said she often sees stories that fall into two camps: the writer says too much or far too little. Each tends to share a root problem—a lack of focus. "I try to get them to refocus their story, to stay on track," said Rivera. "The people who write for us are missionaries and I want them to write from the heart. That's where they begin. But learning to focus their story is the key to good writing."

Whatever route you choose to find your focus, go there. Then all else will follow. Your focus will not only help you write your lead, but it will also play a role in determining what structure your story will take.

Story structure

You may have done stellar research. You may have found the perfect focus. But if you don't know how to order your material around that focus, then no one will find that out. Should you organize your story chronologically? Spatially? In order of importance?

Ordering your material simply means determining what kind of framework would dovetail nicely with your material. Within that framework, though, you have to order your material. This means deciding at which part of the story readers will receive information, a decision that will affect their reaction to the material. (Another way of putting this is that story structure is pivotal to how actively your readers will be involved in your story.)

It's also essential when thinking about story structure to figure out at what point in the story/issue/event you want to begin and at what point you want to finish.

The approach you use will be determined by a variety of factors—the nature of your material, the style your publication favours and where your strengths as a writer lie.

The inverted pyramid

The inverted pyramid is the classical form of news writing. The idea is to get out as much of the news as possible, and to get it out fast. This means providing the most important information within the first few paragraphs. There is no dilly-dallying around, no teasing, no provocation. Instead you say what happened, what's newsworthy, then fill in the details in descending order of importance.

No one knows for sure how or when the inverted pyramid came into being. But it was probably the invention of the telegraph that forced writers to write more economically. The telegraph was fast, but it was also costly, meaning that writers had to pare down their copy. This meant getting the most important information out first and ignoring the embellishments.

Simple news stories are commonly written in the inverted pyramid style. A story begins with a one-paragraph lead of one or perhaps two sentences summing up the essence of the story. The inverted pyramid structure answers any questions readers might have right off the top. The lead is short, typically less than 35 words. Stories aren't organized around ideas or timelines, but around facts. (Wire stories are typically written in this style.) An advantage of this structure for editors is that if a story is too long it can be cut from the bottom without sacrificing essential content.

A lot of people don't like the inverted pyramid style. They argue that it's passé, boring and a turnoff for readers. It can also be difficult for writers insofar as most of our educational background prepared us for writing that builds to a climax. The inverted pyramid structure reverses that process.

In its defence, the inverted pyramid structure allows busy readers to get the news on the fly. It's also a good tool for writers. Having to sum up an entire story in a paragraph is excellent discipline for whatever form your writing takes.

Interestingly, the Internet seems to be playing a role in the comeback of the inverted pyramid. People don't like to read text by scrolling down, so all the essential information is increasingly presented—right off the top—inverted pyramid style.

The chronological story structure

This structure is the most straightforward. You start at the beginning and recount the story through to the end. Unfortunately, it can be just as boring as it sounds. Nevertheless, you can adopt a chronological approach to good effect. Instead of going from A to Z, move back and forth in time. (In cinematic terms, it would be like using a flash-forward or a flash-backward approach.)

Ideally, anyone writing within a chronological structure would play with some flashbacks. For example, you might describe how a father learned about his daughter's death. Then you'd begin a long flashback to retrace the events leading to the murder and the killer's trial.

Or you might introduce someone, then follow the events in his or her life that culminate in a climax, then describe the falling action and, finally, tell the outcome.

The hourglass story structure

The hourglass structure was named by Roy Peter Clark, senior scholar at the Poynter Institute in the U.S. He was struck by how many news stories combined the inverted pyramid structure with a storytelling approach, or narration. He visualized the structure of these stories as that of two pyramids whose points meet—hence the name.

The first part of the hourglass, the top, contains all the important information—just like the inverted pyramid. The middle, though, is referred to as the turn. It signals that a narrative is beginning and orders events chronologically. The final part, known as the narrative, provides detail, dialogue and background information. Put another way, it tells the story.

Nut graf

This story structure begins with an anecdotal lead, followed by sections that amplify the story's focus. A nut graf is the three or four paragraphs within the feature that summarize the focus. It's so called because the nut graf contains the kernel of the story—its essence. It tells readers, in concrete terms, the focus of the story.

The nut graf also connects the opening anecdote to the rest of the story. But more to the point, it tells readers why they should care about the story, why they should read it, and it often hints at how the story is organized. After that essential nut graf, the rest of the story will build on the focus and develop it. Though readers may choose not to continue reading the story, if they get as far as the nut graf, they'll know what the story is about.

The nut graf story structure works best with news features or analytical features.

Leads

There have been times when I've spent more time writing a lead than writing the rest of a story. Why? Well, crafting a lead is a lot of work. In fact, it's the most critical part of anything you write because so much hinges on it. This is because a good lead has to perform many functions.

A good lead must do what it implies—it's got to "hook" readers immediately and lead them into your story. It's got to interest readers and engage them. A lead that lags runs the danger of losing readers.

How's this for an engaging lead? Written by Debra Fieguth, the story entitled "Arctic Revival" ran in the

January–February 2002 edition of *Faith Today*.

> It started like thunder, and at first no one knew what was happening. Moses Kyak, who was operating the sound system, turned the volume off but the noise kept getting louder. Then people began falling down without anyone touching them. James Arreak, who had been leading worship, began to shake. The building began to shake. For about a minute the noise continued to fill the church, like a mighty, rushing wind.

A good lead also has to provide solid information that is both substantial and honest. Never write a lead that promises something it can't deliver. Don't suggest that readers are going to get a lot of exciting material then give them boring, inconsequential facts or details.

In addition, a good lead has to deliver for you, too, insofar as it actually provides an organizing principle for everything that follows. Because it highlights your focus, your lead also helps organize your material. If you don't know what you're trying to say—i.e. what your story is about—you'll end up with two problems: you'll have a bad lead *and* a tough time writing the body of your story.

The reality is, you can't judge your lead unless you understand your central point (your focus). And you can't sail through writing unless you know where you want to go.

If you struggle with writing leads, then you probably neglected an essential early stage of the writing process. Perhaps you set out to write broadly about unformed issues, or topics, rather than about focused ideas. Without a focus, you have no way to organize all the material you've collected. Or perhaps you have a focus, but you didn't take the time to organize your notes and construct a story outline.

All of this helps explain why writing a lead can feel so overwhelming. It incorporates all the hard thinking you have to do to construct a good story.

The worst thing you can do is to create a great lead and then insert a bunch of supporting documentation, add a quotation or two, arrange the chronology and tack on a conclusion. That's just collecting parts and assembling. It makes for disjointed reading and disgruntled readers. (And it doesn't make you feel good about yourself as a professional writer—more like a technician.)

Think of a lead as a device for creating a lasting impression with your readers. Certainly a story about young people hitch-hiking across Canada to attend World Youth Day with the pope is going to have a very different lead from a story about the sexual harassment of female ministers.

What kind of mood do you want to create? Knowing that helps you choose the right words, rhythm and pacing—whatever you need to set that mood. By all means use an anecdote if it's integral to the story. People love stories. Stories draw them in and help them relate to your material. A good lead is an opportunity to introduce a character who will help tell the story, convey its import or illustrate its impact. But if you use an anecdote, then you'll need to return to that person, scene or issue at some other point in the story. This is as much an advantage as a disadvantage, providing a narrative "trail," or potential "book-ends" for your story.

It would be hard to beat a lead like this: *In the beginning God created the heavens and the earth*. It is simple and succinct. It is concrete, not abstract. However, it is also profound and makes you want to read more for the Why? and the How?

Hard news lead

A straight news lead provides a simple summary of story content. It basically tells you what's going to follow. To get all the details, people will have to read to the end. But if they don't have the time, they'll have gotten the essential information from your lead.

A hard news lead is the opening paragraph of a news story or the opening paragraph of a story that gives an account of an event or a set of events that occurred in a specific time and place. Such a lead usually sums up instantly the main point, or points, of the story—and does so with 25–30 words. (In fact, if you read your lead out loud and you have to take a breath to get through it, then it's probably too long.)

Bob Harvey, religion reporter at the *Ottawa Citizen* and a regular columnist for *Faith Today*, said the best thing he learned on the job came from an editor at the *Edmonton Journal*. "He told me to never write a lead that's longer than 25 words," said Harvey. "'Keep it simple,' he said, 'and make it have impact. Because if you don't catch them in that first sentence, then you've lost them.'"

Finally, if in your lead you refer to an event you didn't see or report a statement or assertion based on someone's authority, then you must provide attribution. This simply means that you tell the reader who your source is. Who made that statement or claim? Who described the event in your lead?

Attribution helps to keep your story honest. It is a way of letting readers know exactly who gave you the information they're reading. You aren't pretending to know information you didn't personally see or couldn't possibly know. It also gives readers a basis for deciding the amount of credence they're going to give to that information.

Hard news leads are sometimes called direct, or summary, leads.

Soft news lead

A soft news lead is usually indirect. It doesn't get to the point immediately, the way a hard news lead does. Instead, it uses some device to draw readers down to the main theme, which may be found after two or three, sometimes even 10, paragraphs in feature stories (although that's pushing it).

Here's one, written by Marianne Meed Ward in the September–October 2001 edition of *Faith Today* that ran for five paragraphs before telling readers the focus. The story is entitled "The Alpha-tization of Canada."

The confessions are flying around the room like testimonies at a summer camp meeting.

"I can't love everybody," says Pat rather sheepishly, shifting on her seat in the small book room of Appleby United Church in Burlington, Ont. "I struggle with that. There are really some people I have a hard time loving. I feel that I'm less of a Christian."

"My dad," offers Rebecca by way of commiseration, "lied about having cancer. It's one of the reasons my parents split up. It's hard to forgive what he did."

"What do you do about people like Timothy McVeigh?" adds Bev, referring to the man executed the day before for blowing up a government building in Oklahoma. "That's where I have a real hard time. How can you forgive and love somebody who kills 168 people?"

So the conversation goes. It's the kind of thing you'd expect from some good friends catching up over a cup of coffee. But these are six women who didn't really know each other before they decided to show up at church every Tuesday night for the last nine weeks for something called the Alpha course. Tonight's topic: What about the Church? They're discussing the metaphor of Church as the family of God—with the attendant responsibility to love all its members as you would a brother or sister. They're admitting that it's hard to do....

Anecdotal lead

This is a lead that begins with a vignette. Put another way, it presents a story in compressed form—a story within the story that highlights the writer's focus. The anecdote is usually one or two paragraphs long and is also referred to as a soft, or delayed, lead.

Here's an example from "One child, two cultures" by John Bird in *The United Church Observer*, November 2002.

> Linda Shapiro's adopted Aboriginal daughter, Kelly, ran away from home in her mid-teens and "hit the streets." Now Linda says, "I'm not sure that death could be any harder than that."
>
> In her despair, she says, "I buried Kelly more than once." In real life, "I picked her up more dead than alive more than once. I took her to the hospital more than once." As a white Anglo-Saxon Protestant, she says, "I thought that if you work at it hard enough you can do it." But as she was to discover, "that's just not true." She needed help.

Who? leads

They focus on a person or a group of people. If you're writing a story about a "personality," you're probably going to come up with a Who? lead. Such leads give more prominence to the person than to the event or issue that person is involved with.

Here's an example, from "Baroness Cox warns about loss of freedom" by Laurie McBurney, *ChristianCurrent*, Ottawa edition, June 2002.

> An international human rights worker says religious freedom is at risk in the world today. "There is more religious oppression in the world now than at any other time in history," Baroness Caroline Cox told over 200 people,

including several politicians, assembled on Parliament Hill on May 8.

What? leads

This kind of lead focuses on the event or situation being reported.

Here's an example from "Quebec to give same-sex couples parental rights" by Laura Ieraci in *The Catholic Register*, May 19, 2002: "Quebec's new bill on civil unions will enshrine parental rights for same-sex couples."

When? leads

This is used only when the element of time factors larger than any other element.

Here's an example from "ZAP! Makes a run for the border" by Tara Oetting, *The Canadian Lutheran*, July–August 2001: "Instead of going to Cancun or hanging out with friends or shopping at the mall, 12 youth and three leaders gave up their March Break to tell people about Jesus."

Where? leads

Such leads direct readers to the location of an event. They can be very effective in establishing a mood or an atmosphere.

Here's an example from "A birthday in the north" by Sister Marie Claire Boucher, S.C.S.H. in *Mission Canada*, Fall 2001.

It was the last Sunday of September. The ground wrapped itself in a multicoloured blanket and a light wind made the sun play peak-a-boo between the clouds and the bare trees. In general it was a beautiful cold autumn day in St. Theresa.

Why? and How? leads

These leads help explain events or actions. Often interpretive stories, columns or editorials begin with Why? leads. They're a way for the writer to explain why something happened or what the consequences are.

Here's an example from "Churches, non-profits pressured by insurance companies to get screening protocols in place" by David Harris and Tom Dickey, *Presbyterian Record*, February 2003.

> Fresh from having reached an agreement with Ottawa to limit the church's liability for abuse of native school children last century, Presbyterian congregations are being told they need to develop strict protocols to prevent abuse of children and vulnerable adults today.

Problem leads

Unfortunately, some writers are willing to settle for leads that are less than sparkling. In fact, they'll often be content to run with a dull or boring lead. Or they'll reach for the conventional or the routine, thereby sounding just like every other writer who's ever tackled the subject. Is it laziness? Is it fear? Who knows? But it shouldn't be countenanced. Here are some samples of leads I personally find undesirable.

FORMULA LEAD

I call this the "his or her way" lead. This is the kind of lead that reads, "Wycliffe College will be the site of a new, multimillion dollar library if the director of academic studies has his way."

Sometimes this kind of lead will also include "at least." For example, "Theology students at Regent College are threatening to walk out of classes if they don't get a break from arduous assignments. At least, that's what some honour students are saying."

And sometimes they include both: "Wycliffe College will be the site of a new, multimillion dollar library, at least if the director of academic studies has his way."

UNWIELDY LEAD

It's wise to follow the 25-word structure if you can. If you don't, the upshot can be an overloaded lead—a lead that attempts to cram in too much information. The reality is, you can't put everything that's worth telling into the lead. So don't even try. Stick to your focus and avoid clutter.

QUOTATION LEAD

On a rare occasion a quotation may be the perfect setup for your story. But for the most part, avoid this type of lead. Editors tend to see them as indicative of a lazy writer. Why? Because writers will use them instead of doing the hard work of narrowing the focus themselves.

QUESTION LEAD

These leads should always be avoided. It's far too easy for a question lead to sound like an advertisement. "What makes church council work?" Such a lead lacks intrigue and seems to be a setup for a boring lecture on the machinations of a bureaucracy.

(However, do questions work within the body of a story? Yes. As long as the question is answered immediately and the technique isn't used too often.)

CHEAP LEAD

I also think of this kind of a lead as a desperation lead. It's usually used when writers have absolutely no idea how to get into their story. So they'll begin with, "This is a story about ..."

CLICHÉ LEAD

A common one is this: "It's a parent's worst nightmare..." When a lead like this is used to introduce a harrowing tale of child abduction, it trivializes the feelings of the family and reduces that event to merely one of many.

BACKWARD LEAD

A lead should take readers to the heart of a story immediately. But it's all too common for writers to back into their lead. An example: "Church members voted last month on whether or not to give additional funds to the special relief fund for overseas missions."

This lead doesn't get to the critical issue—which is the result of the vote. Instead, readers are simply told that a vote took place. Here's how it should read: "In an overwhelming show of support, church members voted 172–20 in favour of boosting funding for overseas missions."

NON-NEWS LEAD

When people read the news they want to know what happened. They don't want a lead that doesn't give them any news. For example, "Members of the young people's outreach committee had an opportunity to meet with teenagers from Guatemala last month."

What does this lead tell you? Not much. It does tell you that young people from two geographic zones met. But it doesn't tell you whether they had anything to say to each other—only that they were given the opportunity.

The body of the story

For most people, it's one thing to talk about something, quite another to put it down on paper. It's almost as if the act of writing transforms them from a conversationalist to an academic. If you feel yourself falling prey to that, fight it! The best writing reads the way people talk. It doesn't talk down, but it does present material economically, accessibly and interestingly. Try to visualize a reader or someone you want to communicate with. It helps.

Keep the action moving and connect ideas and paragraphs. Accuracy and sentence clarity are essential. Use quotations, but only if they actually advance your focus, illustrate a point or assertion, or provide insight into a source. (More on quotations in the next chapter.)

Make sure every part of your story works together. One word should set up another. Each sentence should do the same. And your conclusion should be a logical upshot of all that's gone before.

Don't be afraid to plunge in. Depending on time, you can always make major revisions. The important thing is to get started and to trust yourself.

The end of the story

Think of writing a feature as akin to serving guests a special meal. When it is over, you hope they'll feel satisfied, content to move on with their lives after having spent a stimulating time with a friend who obviously cares about their issues and concerns.

How you end your story will play a critical role in the impression the story makes on readers.

One very effective technique is to begin and end with approximately the same idea, phrase, or description as you began. It serves to connect, and it unifies your material—which is why it's often referred to as the circle technique. Return to the opening anecdote or character, for example.

Or you could end with a "kicker." This captures the idea

that anyone who reads through to the end of a story gets a reward. It could be in the form of a quotation, a bit of humour, an image or an idea. Whatever the device, it should provoke readers to further thought.

Perhaps more important than knowing what a kicker is, however, is grasping what it isn't. A kicker is *not* a conclusion. It doesn't sum up the story, provide a moral to it, or impart an opinion. Neither a news story nor a feature story is commentary. They shouldn't end as if they were. You are not expected to resolve an issue or provide closure, but merely to present a fair and complete account of its complexities.

The final step: Changing/revising/ reworking/rewriting

Though good writing may read as if the words flowed straight from a writer's heart onto the page, the best writing has been worked and reworked and reworked again. In short, the writer has been brutal. This is hard. Most of us tend to think that every word we write is precious. How can we possibly cut any out? But if you strive for excellence, then you're going to have to learn to take a machete to your work. Often that cutting and slashing is what's needed to bring out the latent potential of an article.

Perhaps cutting and slashing and rewriting are difficult because writing is so personal. It's a creative act that comes out of your innermost self. Consciously or unconsciously, each time you write you're revealing a part of yourself in a public way. Cutting out copy can feel like an amputation or a personal rejection.

Another reason people may resist revising is that they severely underestimate the writing process. They tend to think of it as something quick and easy. They don't understand how much practice is required. Yet anything that is worthwhile comes about through practice. Your church choir doesn't automatically know how to blend and combine their voices to make beautiful music. They work at it. In fact, they'll spend hours on it—all for the sake of one piece of music on a Sunday morning. Why should writing be any different?

Perhaps the task would be easier if, instead of thinking of it as revising, you thought of it as "envisioning again." Ask yourself what you could do to tell your story more simply, more plainly, more accurately, more eloquently. Work at bringing your story closer to your original concept. Reread *everything*. This may result in cutting out parts. It may involve combining others. Ask yourself if you have been faithful to your focus. If not, start again.

Even the most experienced writers don't get the right order, tone or quality on the first go-round. In fact, they are probably their own harshest critics because they've learned through time that a really good story involves cutting and slashing, even re-envisioning, if necessary.

Be brutal. Sometimes you may end up cutting out pages of work—work that represents hours, if not days, of effort. This can be very discouraging. But it doesn't have to be. It really is part of the writing process. Also, think of it this way. You've got two editors—an internal one and an external one. Wouldn't you prefer to do the initial cutting and the slashing?

In fact, your work will be only as good as the extent to which you trust and work well with both editors. Give the first few drafts to your internal editor. Only when it's passed that test should you hand it over to your external one. As hard as it is, try to read your own work objectively. Changing hats (from writer to editor) can really help. And if this works for you, even go so far as to pretend that it isn't your story you're reading. Take yourself out of the picture completely.

Hannah Moor said she once had a story rejected and was so devastated that she phoned another writer friend to ask for suggestions on reworking it. "What she said to me was, 'You figure it out.' Oh, I hated her that day!" said Moor. "But that was the best thing she could possibly have said. *I* needed to do the work." Another time she had a story returned; she scrutinized it carefully then took a paragraph out of the middle and made it her lead. It sold immediately.

It also helps if you can afford to let some time lapse between writing a story and reading it. The pause removes some of that emotional attachment. Reading your story out loud can also point to problem areas. Finally—and perhaps this is just me—I need to work from a hard copy. I simply don't catch everything on a computer screen. Find out what works best for you and then do it consistently.

Remember that the object of revision isn't to lower your self-esteem or to create a "make work" project. The idea is to make your story more powerful, to ensure that everything you've written is on focus and is woven together as tightly and seamlessly as a haute couture outfit. This means asking tough questions of both your work and yourself.

It means checking for certain essentials. Does your lead work? Is it catchy? Does it hook the reader? Did you stick to your focus? Have you written in a plain style, using words that are both precise and accurate? Have you answered the five Ws and H? Have you verified all your facts? Is your voice evident? Have you made any style errors, spelling errors, grammatical errors? And finally, does everything work together as a whole?

Answering this last question means examining how words fit together, how sentences mesh and whether paragraphs flow together nicely. It also involves ascertaining whether you've signposted your work well enough. Have you provided enough of a road map for readers taking this journey? If not, where should you signal transitions and changes?

Once you've answered all those questions to your satisfaction, then your story is probably ready for your "second" editor.

Your editor and you

You may have heard the maxim, "Every writer needs an editor." Well, it's true. And a good editor is worth her weight in gold. A good editor loves language, loves the challenge of communicating well, and enjoys working with writers to improve their copy. A good editor knows his readership, has lots of hands-on experience and is the final pair of eyes to see your story before it goes to press. As such, it's the editor's job to make sure your story has no factual errors, sticks to its focus, is written accurately, fairly and with style, leaves no questions unanswered (i.e. has no "holes") and meets length requirements.

Your editor will trim your story if it's too long or if it's overwritten. If it has major problems, your editor may send it back to you for further research and/or rewriting.

It's important to cultivate a good relationship with the editors you work with. They are professionals, so take advantage of their expertise. Learn from them. Don't expect praise. Remember it's their job to zero in on the problem areas.

If you disagree with changes they suggest, discuss your differences. But don't be a prima dona. Above all, be respectful. And when they help you, express your appreciation. The published story may have your name on the byline, but you should recognize that, ultimately, it is always a collaborative effort.

If you're working with an editor for the first time, remember that it will take time for your editor to learn to trust you. You will have to earn that trust by producing accurate, clean copy that meets professional standards. However, once you prove yourself, you'll probably find that interventions occur less and less often.

If you ever find yourself in the position of editing someone else's work, try to remember what it was like to be the writer. Don't change copy for the sake of changing copy— i.e. to show who's boss! It's important not to rob a writer of his or her "voice." And when changes are needed, try to discuss them with respect.

Summing up

The bottom line in any story form is to know who you're writing for, what your focus is and what story structure best suits your topic. Invest the time to find a captivating lead. Then, write from your heart.

Writing Devices

Writing is work. Hard work. Writing is also something that a lot of people think they can do—sometimes just because they think they have interesting ideas to share. Or, because they had theological training or went to university, they often assume they can write. And, if they spend any time reading good writing, it's easy to be duped into believing that writing is an effortless process. "So, how hard can it be?' they wonder. "I'm sure I could have written *that*."

Well, there's writing and then there's writing. And just because someone *wants* to write, it doesn't mean he or she *can* write.

For publications that run on a shoestring, it's tempting to accept copy from anyone who offers to put pen to paper. Unfortunately, the result can be a story that no one wants to read (although a sense of obligation is a great motivator). Other unwelcome results are a frustrated editor and time spent reworking and rewriting! Bad writing, like cheap art, is a bad investment.

Writing is both an art and a vocation. As such, it requires discipline, imagination, innovation, apprenticeship and the commitment to treat it as a lifelong practice. Whether you feel *called* to write or you think you *want* to write or your struggling publication *needs* you to write, there are certain tricks you can learn to hone your writing skills. And the effort is worth it; those skills will be with you the rest of your life.

You'll need to write good, clear sentences that are grammatically correct, contain no misspelled words and are in an active voice. Why are these skills essential? Because no matter how important your topic or how knowledgeable you are, if you can't write in readable prose, none of that significance or expertise will count for much. No one will read you.

"Being able to express yourself in clear sentences is something people should work at," said Harold Jantz, former editor of *Mennonite Brethren Herald* and founding editor of *ChristianWeek*. "It's a struggle for me, too. Sometimes I wonder what I've written. But beginning writers should try to follow the fundamental rules: to write clearly, to use active verbs and images that catch readers, and with sentences and paragraphs that hang together."

How hard you work to learn these skills, and how hard you work at applying them will determine whether you develop into the kind of writer that people respect and find a joy to read. Ultimately, there's only one way to be a writer— to think and to work like one.

Here are some useful writing devices.

Plain language

Sometimes people assume, when they're writing for the Christian press, that they have to write effusively. But the most powerful writing is often the most economic. This involves using just the right word to convey what you want to say. It means not using a $2 word when a 50-cent word will do. It means choosing words that jump to the heart of the matter.

It doesn't mean "dumbing down" your copy, or writing at a Grade 8 level. The assumption behind "dumbing down" is that you know more than your readers do and, what's more, they probably aren't able to handle what you know. "Dumbing down" does a disservice to the truth and underestimates people's capacity to be stretched, as well as their ability to deal with the truth you have uncovered.

Plain language involves cutting out clutter and translating jargon into accessible language. It means providing just the right amount of explanation to get your point across. Too little or too much will turn off readers.

It also means eliminating redundancies and using metaphors and images that work, that entice people to enter into the world of your story and to stick with it to the end. It means using grammar correctly, spelling words precisely and following a consistent writing style.

Following the subject–verb–object rule can help you write plainly. "The church purchased a new organ," is clearer (and more active) than, "The organ was purchased by the church." Also try to keep your average sentence length short. If you read a lot of good writing, you'll soon notice that sentences average around 17 words. Sentences of up to 35 words can work if they flow well. But don't try to push it beyond that. You'll simply confuse or lose readers.

However, bear in mind that an important way to add interest to your story is to vary the length of your sentences. If you build all your sentences with a subject–verb–object structure and run them all the same length, the result will be deadly. The power of words often comes, after all, not just by choosing the right ones, but from putting them together rhythmically in sentences of different length and varying the order of your sentences.

Clear writing

People can't read your mind. They have only your words to help them follow your logic. One of the easiest ways to write clearly is to write the way you talk—conversationally. And get to the point as directly and quickly as possible. One way to do that is to have a clear focus and to stick to it.

People who write unclear sentences often leave me with the impression they don't understand their subject. Conversely, it's a lot easier to write clearly if you have a firm understanding of your subject.

Think of your story as a journey you're inviting readers to take with you. To get them to come along, you've got to tell them where you're going. Then you have to take them there by the most interesting and the shortest route. But don't assume that just because you told them at the beginning where they're going, they'll remember. They could become confused, disoriented. So keep sign posting. Bill Fledderus, senior editor at *Faith Today* said he sees this kind of problem all the time. "A significant number of writers fail to indicate to the reader where the article is headed," he said, "and then they fail to guide the reader along the way."

Also, continually ask yourself the So what? question. Why should anyone care about this story? Why should people read it? Asking those questions helps you write more clearly because, by answering them, you will hone in on the essentials.

Be specific. A good rule of thumb is to follow every generality with a specific. And use concrete nouns, verbs and modifiers. They add energy. Abstractions simply float off into another time zone. And though you might have been told never to begin a sentence with "and," "but" or "because," the practice is generally accepted in journalism as long as those words don't begin the first sentence of a paragraph. They are used because they contribute to shorter and easier-to-understand sentences. However, use only if necessary and don't overdo them.

Try not to get mired in details. It's an easy trap to fall into if you've done good research. You'll have so many of them. More to the point, you'll find most of them genuinely interesting. But if the details don't support your focus, leave them out. Think plain and think simple. And don't raise questions you don't answer. You don't want readers to make their way through your story only to feel short-changed and frustrated at the end.

Unfortunately, many would-be writers think writing for a Christian publication means adopting a religious style of writing. "But piety in every word tends to bog down both the writer and the reader," said Ian Adnams, editor of *The Canadian Lutheran*. "Writers should have a good sense of their story, but they don't need to be reverent about it. In fact, I often paraphrase Scripture in the vernacular. It jars people. But this is good because I want people to think about their faith. I always treat material with respect, but I think we should aim to engage readers, to bring people in."

Kenn Ward, former editor of *Canada Lutheran*, said he receives a lot of pieces that "use religious clichés, hackneyed religious jargon and predictable religious images. If I glaze over and yawn," he said, "then I know that my readers will react the same way."

For her part, Hannah Moor said she's seen stories that "read like a hymnbook"—and she doesn't mean this as a compliment! At the same time, she's encountered readers who expected the same from her. For example, a man once informed her that her writing wasn't Christian enough. "I told him I didn't need to mention God on every page," she said. "To me, what's important is writing about the things that He's interested in—our questions and our problems. Every word I put on paper is Christian writing."

Moor is speaking about an important truth in writing—the implicit is often more honest and convincing than the explicit. Just as practicing one's faith can be more influential than preaching or talking about it.

Showing, not telling

Professionals are writers even when they aren't writing. This means they see the world through the eyes of a writer. They pay attention to their five senses, to soaking in everything around them, to observing the ways in which people live their lives and interact with others. They follow the news. They try to understand the underlying meaning behind current events.

All of this is critical because one of the most challenging things you will confront in writing is to evoke images, to suggest. This is quite the opposite from preaching a sermon. In journalistic terms, it's called "show, don't tell." Don't tell readers about redemption. Instead, describe a situation in which a life was transformed. People will read it. You will touch them and, if you write well, you will awaken something in them.

The same goes for feelings. Instead of telling readers how to feel about a person, an issue or a situation, choose words that describe accurately what you see and leave them to decide for themselves how they feel.

"Show, don't tell" is an important maxim for another reason. If you "tell" people something, you're asking them to trust your perception. You're asking them to see things your way. If, instead, you "show" them something, if you paint a scene effectively, then you are asking them to trust their own reactions.

Still, there are places where the "show, don't tell" rule breaks down. You won't always want to always "show" and

126

never "tell." There will be times when the best way to keep a story rolling is by summarizing. You'll have to judge when to use it and when not to. It will all depend on the type of story you're writing and the material you have at hand.

Use summaries sparingly, however. Besides confusing commentary with reporting, they can seem to suggest that your readers are too dumb to grasp the point of your story. If you've told your story well, there's no need to tack a moral onto the end. You're neither teaching nor preaching. You're taking readers into a world inhabited by people grappling with the issue you're writing about. Let them encounter diversity of thought—and come to their own conclusions.

Precision

English is a rich and living language. Don't settle for the first word that pops into your mind. Think hard about each word you use. Is it the best one available? Is there another word to convey the same meaning, one that would be more effective, more concise, more energetic? Buy a thesaurus and keep it nearby so it becomes easy for you to check for synonyms. Keep the *Canadian Oxford Dictionary* on hand for precise meanings.

Be careful about how you use both adjectives and adverbs. Good ones add meaning to your story. If they don't, be ruthless. Eliminate them. The same goes for imagery. It's too easy to get cute, so use it sparingly. Imagery should be used to illuminate, not to show off or exaggerate.

In her book, *The Cloister Walk*, Kathleen Norris puts it well. "Even when the psalms are at their most ecstatic, they convey holiness not with abstraction but with images from the world we know: rivers clap their hands, hills dance like yearling sheep."

Adjectives

Adjectives can go a long way toward evoking a mood or creating a picture. But don't overdo them, because adjectives can be tricky. They can come across as judgmental. Here's a hypothetical example: Gisele Lamond is breaking new ground in Christian music with her big voice, big heart and equally big presence. Standing nearly six feet tall and carrying the weight of a overfed sumo wrestler, the singer has been offered a deal with a major U.S. label.

The judicious use of adjectives can make your writing more concrete. Don't simply refer to the "church" in your feature story. Tell your readers what kind of church it is—frame, stucco, brick, fortress-like, diminutive. If you are writing about things that can be seen or heard or measured, describe them in concrete terms with strong adjectives.

Specific is better than vague. Here's an example from "Letting go of the real estate" by Mike Milne in *The United Church Observer*, April 2002.

> Pamela Morrison looks over the tidy, sun-swept church hall, its walls decorated with tea-pot-lined shelves and frame prints of Celtic knot-work and crosses. Tables are set and ready for tomorrow's traditional Cape Breton dinner of marragh—an oatmeal-based sausage.

Don't use adjectives to repeat the obvious. If an event is self-evidently tragic, you can demean it by describing it as such.

Anecdotes

Anecdotes are important. They keep a story moving and keep readers captivated. They also help to illustrate character traits. In fact, the essence of a good article is the anecdote, a small story that shows a person or a group of people in action. Anecdotes work best if you put them early in the story.

Anecdotes matter because they are about real people. They give your readers someone to identify with or to contrast themselves with. They involve the reader.

How do you get them? You talk to people. You ask them for an anecdote to illustrate a point or an experience. You can even ask leading questions, depending on the subject of your story. For example, "What was the strangest experience you had on the mission?" or "What was your most memorable experience when lobbying against the bill on Parliament Hill?"

Analogy

An analogy says to the reader, "You know what I mean? It's as if …" And then a comparison follows. A good analogy helps convey a mood, an appearance, an experience to drive a point home in a concrete way.

For example, I once read a medical story that compared an aneurysm on an artery to a bump on a tire about to blow. That is an image I'm never going to forget. It lives on because it was dramatic and accurate, and it created an image I could relate to.

Analogies can enrich a story by adding colour and drama. However, they must be appropriate and they must be good. If you don't find that an analogy comes easily, then concentrate on making your point another way.

Metaphor

A metaphor is different from an analogy, although at first glance it may appear to be similar. A metaphor is symbolic of a quality in another, very different thing. It compares one thing to another without the use of "like" or "as."

Norris refers to metaphor as "valuable to us precisely

because it is not vapid, not a blank word such as 'reality' that has no grounding in the five senses. Metaphor draws on images from the natural world, from our senses, and from the world of human social structures, and yokes them to psychological and spiritual realities in such a way that we're often left gasping; we have no way to fully explain a metaphor's power, it simply is."

Though highly effective if used well, metaphors are difficult to describe. However, my *Oxford Dictionary* refers to "those beautiful metaphors in scripture, where life is termed a pilgrimage."

Humour

Good humour is hard to beat. A point can be made, seemingly effortlessly and without offence, through the effective use of humour. And in the right place and with the right rhythm, humour can move your story along. But humour is tough. What's funny to one person isn't to another. Besides, humour is hard to write. If it doesn't come naturally, don't attempt it.

Active voice

It's worth putting a lot of effort into using active, rather than passive, voice in all your writing. Writing in the active voice adds power and energy; passive writing does the exact opposite. An example: "Votes were cast for the new slate of officers," is passive. Better to write, "Delegates elected a new slate of officers."

Wherever possible, use active verbs. Make the subject of your sentence do something, rather than letting something be done to it. For example, "The pastor preached on Paul's letter to the Romans" is stronger than, "A sermon on Paul's letter to the Romans was given by the pastor." The first is active, the second passive.

Another way to think of active writing is to make your sentences declarative. Declarative is not, however, the same as opinionated. It simply means making your point concretely and succinctly.

Attribution

It's easy to get tired of using "says" or "said" in your stories. They seem so common, so plain. There will probably come a time when you'll think they must bore readers just as much as they bore you. But if you carry that line of thinking to its next step, you'll start replacing "says" and "said" with such verbs as "expostulated," "exclaimed," "declared," "averred," "remarked," "admitted." This is not a good idea. Any of those variations has subtle tones and meanings that can convey a message quite different from the one you intend.

It's also best to avoid using the words "according to." Why? You are shifting the focus away from what is being said to the person saying it. This is especially true if you begin a sentence that way. The only time to use "according to" is when you need to refer to an inanimate object. For example, "The controversial debate will continue next month, according to *The Catholic Register*."

In fact, you can never overuse "says" or "said." Think of them as a form of punctuation, an essential way of identifying sources. Unlike most of their replacements, they are neutral. However, if someone is actually shouting, whispering or hissing, then say so. Otherwise, stick to "says" or "said."

Also, if you want to write that someone "thinks," "believes" or "feels" something, then write "says" or "said" before them. You don't actually know how other people feel or what they actually think or believe. You know only what they tell you. So if they say they think such and such, then write that "John Doe said he thinks such and such," not simply "John Doe thinks such and such." The exception is when you have a paragraph or longer passage in which it is clear that all quotations and paraphrases arise from a particular source. It then becomes cumbersome, even distracting, for the reader to repeatedly encounter "he said he thinks." The point is to be clear that this information is coming from the source; in some situations it is not necessary to repeatedly make that point.

And be careful not to confuse the meaning of those words. They are not interchangeable. Someone who "thinks" something is expressing an opinion. If the person "believes" something, he or she is referring to a conviction or a principle. But if someone "feels" something, that refers to emotions, to sense of touch, to health or to state of mind.

Quotations

People like to hear people talk. If you're writing a profile, let readers listen in on what that person has to say. But don't use quotations for simple pleasantries or small talk. In fact, don't use a quotation at all unless it says something important. Each quotation that's used should be especially meaningful. Avoid the pedestrian. Also avoid paraphrasing a quotation when leading into it. And put good quotations up high in your stories.

Quotations, of course, aren't used only in profile writing. If you're writing about an event or a thing or an idea and you refer to an authority, then open that person's mouth and let him or her speak. However—and this is *really* important—be selective. No matter how good the quotations are, no article should be overwhelmingly composed of quotations. It's boring. Besides, you can usually present a source's thoughts more economically in your writing than by quoting.

"Many writers want to put in as much direct material from their source as there is space for," said Bill Fledderus. "But the result gives the reader the feeling the writer has lost control and has become a mouthpiece for the source."

That is not a situation you want to find yourself in. You are driving the bus. It's your job to keep control of it.

The Canadian Press Stylebook calls quotations "the lifeblood of any story. They put rosiness into the cheeks of the palest stories. They add credibility, immediacy and punch."

Quotations are direct evidence. The words are coming "from the horse's mouth," as it were. They should be used to buttress your story.

The stylebook also points out that quotations can also bring grief to both writers and editors if anyone "plays loose" with them. So bear in mind that a direct quotation conveys the *exact* words of the speaker. However, it is generally considered acceptable to remove verbal mannerisms (the "ahs" and "uhs"), to clean up seriously incorrect grammar (unless it's critical to conveying the personality of the person) and to eliminate meaningless repetitions. Direct quotations add colour and life to stories. They also make good kickers.

Here's a direct quotation from the December 2002 issue of the *Anglican Journal*. "'For some years, we have been preoccupied with litigation. We can now return to our principal occupation, serving God and God's world in ministries of healing, reconciliation and compassion,' said Archbishop Peers."

Unfortunately, not everyone speaks so clearly and concisely. In that case, perhaps instead of using a direct quotation, a partial quotation would work better. That is when you use fragments of a person's words. In that case, your story might read, "Archbishop Peers says an agreement with the federal government limiting the church's liability over Indian residential schools will allow Anglicans 'to return to our principal occupation, serving God and God's world.'"

There will also be times when you will want to remove words from the text, in which case you should use ellipsis. Here's an example in a quotation from the Anglican Archbishop of Canterbury, George Carey: "'The Church of England is poised with the rest of the Anglican Communion in standing firm on traditional morality and... it's my view that we shift from that at our peril,' he said." (*Anglican Journal*, December 2002)

There may be times when you will use a quotation that requires clarification or additional information. In that case, don't hesitate to interrupt the quotation with the material. However, it's essential that readers know that the inserted information comes from you, not the source, so enclose it within square brackets. Do not use parentheses, because those indicate that the parenthetical material is from the source.

For example, suppose you know from your interview or the surrounding material of a quotation from a print source that your quoted source is referring to *The War Cry*, but how is the reader to know that? You could make the reference clear this way: "The news that we are operating in a deficit situation was first published in the July 2002 edition [of *The War Cry*]," said the head of the building fund. The added material must be inserted in such a way that the quotation is still a grammatically complete sentence.

Note, however, that using brackets to provide explanations, clarifications, directions or missing information should be done sparingly and the bracketed material should be brief.

Finally, there may be times when you simply want to paraphrase what someone said. This means you won't put any of the words within quotation marks. Drawing from the above example, you might write, "The Anglican Archbishop of Canterbury, George Carey, says the Church of England will stand firm on traditional morality as any departure could prove dangerous."

If a quotation continues beyond one sentence, try to identify the source in the first sentence. Readers shouldn't have to wait too long to find out whose perspective they're getting. When you've provided attribution in the first paragraph, there is generally no need to provide further attribution in the second.

Also, when you're attributing a quotation to someone, use "Smith says," or "Smith said," instead of "said Smith," or "says Smith." The latter is awkward and isn't the way people generally talk. Titles should be placed after a person's name— unless the title is one that would normally be used in greeting or addressing the person. For example, "Archbishop Michael Kelly," not "Michael Kelly, archbishop of Norfolk."

When should you use quotations? For opinions, for emotional emphasis, for revelation (about a person's character), for more than factual content. A quotation is most justified when it illustrates some attribute unique to the person being quoted. (See Chapter 7, on ethics, to examine if, and when, to quote people anonymously.)

Characterization

Readers not only want to hear people talk, they want to see them. So paint a picture. However, there's more to characterization than description. This is when "show, don't tell" really works. You can provide considerable insight into character by showing a person in action, relating to people, or by presenting a person through the reactions and comments of others.

And, as much as descriptive language is important, tread carefully. If you're five feet tall in your stocking feet and you're interviewing someone who's five feet eight inches, you might be inclined to describe him as tall. But in relation to someone who's six feet four inches, he isn't.

Analogies may be helpful in characterization. For example, "Bethel Church is a David to the local bingo hall's Goliath."

Diversity

When someone complained that *Canada Lutheran* wasn't representing the diversity of voices within the church, Kenn Ward took it seriously. "People said if they were in the minority, then they weren't heard," he said. "So I created opportunities for dissenting voices to be heard. At first, people were hostile. But when they found I actually wanted to help them make their case, they were no longer strident."

Ward opened the door to diversity, an essential component of effective reporting and writing. Your stories should reflect the same diversity of voices, faces and viewpoints that exists within your readership. If they don't, then you're depriving your readers of the full picture, of the richness that exists in humanity. Worse still, you may be contributing to the marginalization of members of the community.

Muriel Duncan, editor of *The United Church Observer*, said she takes the attitude that the magazine belongs to everyone, that it must be inclusive "because we're all God's children." And if you believe that, she said, "then all God's children should have a place at the table. This belief informs how I assemble the magazine and who I want it to be here for.

Duncan said that having an ethnic minorities council in the church helps provide insight into how different levels of inclusion might work. Ten years or so ago, for example, she said, *The United Church Observer* wrote *about* minorities. "Then they said they didn't *see* themselves in the magazine. Now the discussion revolves around whether they have a *voice*. The problem is they are a small minority in the church, so in everyday coverage they might not be there. The coverage has to be intentional. Also, because many don't feel comfortable writing in English, we have to search to find ways to include them."

The situation, Duncan said, is not that dissimilar to that of women many years earlier. They'd argued that they were absent in the magazine. They lobbied for change. Their concerns were addressed. Changes occurred.

"We try to see everything as inclusive. We believe we're called to do it. But," she added, "we also have a journalistic notion of news. We don't want to be a textbook!"

It's not difficult to write interesting well-written stories that are inclusive. But as Duncan said, doing so probably begins with the serious intent to do so, to making the effort to reach out and talk to males and females, young and old, able-bodied and disabled, from diverse communities.

When you're writing, examine your words to determine whether you are inadvertently perpetuating stereotypes and clichés. Are you using language that is inclusive to describe people with accuracy and care? Or are you being insensitive to their reality?

Inclusive language doesn't adopt an external or dominant vantage point, but is implicitly egalitarian. It avoids any presumption of "we" versus "they."

Transitional devices

You may occasionally find yourself in a pickle. You've ended a thought in one paragraph and now need to begin a completely new train of thought in the next. This is a dangerous moment. If you blithely skip on to the next thought without any bridge or link between the two, the effect can be jarring. And if you upset your readers often enough, you'll lose them. You need to look for ways to keep your copy flowing smoothly by providing some kind of transition, or hook, to keep readers on board.

Here are some examples of transitional words and phrases when you're trying to show addition: again, equally important, furthermore, in addition, first, last. If you're looking for transitional words to express contrast, you could use such words and phrases as these: yet, but, however, nevertheless, on the contrary, still, in spite of.

Transitional words and phrases to express the passing of time could include these: afterward, immediately, in the meantime, meanwhile, presently, shortly, since. And to summarize, you could use such words and phrases as these: in brief, on the whole, in conclusion.

And in conclusion

There is no substitute for being there—for being where your story is unfolding or for conducting an interview live. If you develop your observation skills, your writing is bound to be better.

Use examples and anecdotes. They put information in a form that readers can readily relate to. They help to make the abstract concrete. They also make your assertions more believable. You shouldn't be writing, "He loved his congregation." Write about how the pastor demonstrated love for the congregation.

Explain—and then explain some more. Remember that you had the benefit of researching what you're writing about. Your readers haven't. So drop the jargon. Don't let the language of academics or theologians get in the way of a reader's comprehension. By all means, convey what your sources said. But if they said it verbosely, jargonistically or bureaucratically, then paraphrase.

Keep things moving. Use action verbs and avoid passive language. A good way to do this is to use short sentences and concrete and familiar words.

5

Writing Style and Grammar

Style

Editors want their publications to be readable and accessible to their readership. Good writing is an essential aspect of that. So is style. Style refers to the way stories are put together. There needs to be consistency in spelling, sentence structure, word usage, paragraphing, punctuation, the use of titles, and so on. *The Canadian Press Stylebook* is the standard reference Canadian journalists have used for more than half a century. Most secular newsrooms follow it to one degree or another, although many have developed in-house style guides as well. Though no two style guides are identical, each is internally consistent.

Some basic elements of CP style include writing in short paragraphs; using simple punctuation (but using it properly); identifying people by first and last name on first reference, then by last name only after that; not using titles such as Mr., Mrs. or Ms.; and spelling out numbers up to nine, using numerals for 10 and above.

Although it may take time to develop a comfort level with

The CP Stylebook because it's a complicated book to navigate, it is an excellent resource. So is its accompanying handbook, *CP Caps and Spelling*. Find out what style your publication follows. (For example, find out if your publication wants you to put "-30-" at the end of your stories. That's the traditional notation used by journalists to indicate that the story has come to an end.) Most periodicals follow some form of CP style. If so, buying the stylebook and taking the time to learn what's in it will be worth your while.

Grammar

Language changes and style evolves. Witness the fact that *The Canadian Press Stylebook* is now in its 12th edition. But some things haven't changed—at least not yet. I'm referring to the need to write sentences that are grammatically correct. This can pose a problem insofar as you may feel you can't write in a way that's both conversational and grammatically correct.

Many people commit grammatical errors when they're talking. The one that bothers me the most is also one of the most common: use of a singular verb with a plural noun. For example, "There's four ways to approach this problem." If you want to quote someone who speaks that way, then paraphrase. Don't compound the error by repeating it.

This section of the book will deal with some of the most obvious grammatical problem areas. It isn't exhaustive. It can't be. Many fine grammar books on the market cover that ground. (Two of the classics continue to provide excellent advice: *The Elements of Style* by Strunk and White, and *Writing Well* by William Zinsser.) So get yourself a good one and refer to it regularly until you become confident that you've mastered the complexities and intricacies of using the English language. If you want to be a wordsmith, this is something you *must* master.

Frequently confused words

ITS, IT'S

It's easy not to make this mistake. Simply remember that "it's" is a contraction for "it is." Without the apostrophe, "its" is a possessive pronoun. Reading your sentence out loud can usually help you decide whether you should use "it's" or "its."

THEY'RE, THEIR, THERE

"They're" is a contraction for they are. For example, "They're my best youth leaders."

"Their" is a plural possessive pronoun. For example, "Members of the choir will be shown their seats during the next rehearsal."

"There" is used to refer to a place, a point in time or as an exclamation. For example, "The editor told him his story should begin there." Or "There! I knew you could write an engaging lead."

PAST, PASSED

"Passed" is a verb. For example, "She passed the time by reading post-graduate theological texts."

"Past" can be used as several parts of speech, but never as a verb. For example, "There were times in my past when I felt writing was too hard to pursue as a vocation."

THAT, WHICH

"That" and "which" are not interchangeable. *The CP Stylebook* points out that "'that' is generally used when the clause is essential to the noun it defines or narrows the topic." For example, "The revival meetings that began last week at the Fair Grounds will close on the weekend." It's not just any revival meetings but those that began last week.

A phrase introduced by "which" gives a reason or adds

new element. For example, "The revival meetings, which cost $25,000 to launch, have attracted hundreds of people from the outlying area." As the stylebook puts it, "'Which' clauses generally need commas, 'that' clauses don't."

To, Too, Two

"To" is a preposition if it's followed by a noun or a pronoun subject. For example, "Synod members are going to a retreat this weekend." When followed by a verb, "to" is part of the infinitive form. For example, "Mary Douglas plans to enter the convent after she graduates from university."

"Too" is an adverb that means "in addition," or "extremely." For example, "The choir leader will go, too." Or "The public outcry against the controversial textbook was too much for the local trustees to handle."

"Two" means a pair of, a couple of or simply one plus one. For example, "Tyndale College will upgrade two sessional lecturers to tenure-track positions next month."

Affect, Effect

"Affect," as a verb, means "to influence." For example, "He hoped to affect the outcome of the vote by attracting new delegates."

When "effect" is used as a noun, it means "result." For example, "How much of an effect the new delegates had on the outcome of the vote remains to be seen." But "effect" can also be used as a verb, when the meaning is "to cause." For example, "The Primate's World Development and Relief Fund has effected many changes in outreach programs."

About, Almost, Approximately, Around

"About" means "nearly" or "approximately." For example, "About 1,000 people attended the inauguration of the new president."

"Almost" means "very nearly, but not more than" or "not exactly." For example, "The theft of 20 rare books from the library went undetected for almost a month."

"Approximately" means "nearly exact" or "almost alike." For example, "Approximately 500 people attended the candlelight vigil."

"Around" means "all sides of." For example, "The fundraising event requires each participant to run around the track 20 times." *Never* use "around" to refer to people. For example, "Around 5,000 people showed up for the anti-war demonstration."

ACCEPT, EXCEPT

"Accept" means "to receive." For example, "The director of the women's missionary society accepted a $1,000 contribution from an anonymous donor."

"Except" means to "exclude" or "omit." For example, "Every church member, except those who were asked in person, will be mailed an invitation."

ADVICE, ADVISE

"Advice" is a noun and it means "counsel." For example, "The writer took the editor's advice and changed her focus."

"Advise" is a verb and means "to counsel" or "to give advice." For example, "Several deacons advised the youth director to get more training."

ALTOGETHER, ALL TOGETHER

"Altogether" means "wholly." For example, "At his retirement dinner, the minister said that parish work is altogether different from what it was when he began 35 years ago."

"All together" means every person or thing at the same place. For example, "The last time the founding members were all together was at the summer retreat of 1998."

AMONG, BETWEEN

When two people, places or things are involved, use "between." For example, "The contest between Joe Smart and Martha Daniels is expected to be close."

When the number is three or more, use "among." For example, "The new president will probably divide the responsibilities among the administrators, faculty and student representatives."

AMOUNT, NUMBER

"Amount" can't be counted. For example, "The amount of advertising that people are subjected to on a daily basis is amazing."

"Number" refers to a quantity of people or things that can be counted. For example, "The number of international reporters covering the Pope's visit to Canada won't be known for another week." Do not write, "A large amount of people attended the event."

DISINTERESTED, UNINTERESTED

"Disinterested" describes someone who is impartial, who has no interest in the outcome. For example, "The committee is seeking 10 disinterested people to determine the future of the alternative school."

"Uninterested" describes a bored person, someone who isn't interested in what's going on. For example, "The minister noticed that a number of his parishioners appeared uninterested in his sermon."

OVER, MORE THAN

"Over" refers to positions or places. For example, "With their hands over their hearts, the young people welcomed the visiting Nicaraguans." "More than" refers to a number or an amount. For example, "The largest choir at the weekend retreat will have more than 55 singers" (not "over 55 singers").

PROPHECY, PROPHESY

"Prophecy" is a noun and it means a "prediction." For example, "Many prophecies in the Bible have been fulfilled."

"Prophesy" is a verb and it means "to predict." For example, "That New Age spiritualist is prophesying that aliens will soon appear on Earth." Neither word should be used in place of "estimate" or "guess."

Redundancies

If you want to write simply and clearly, you've got to clean up the clutter. This means eliminating redundancies. It's easy to let them slip into your stories because so many people use them in their everyday speech. Here are some of the more common redundancies:

"Packed to capacity." Well, capacity is as full as you can get. If a stadium is packed, then it's packed to capacity.

"Single most"—as in "The single most frequent suggestion was to offer more music," or "It's the single biggest issue to arise in a decade." But if something is the biggest, or the most, then you don't need to add the word "single" to it.

"Unique" is, quite simply, unique. It's one of a kind by definition. Something or someone can't be "very unique," "pretty unique" or "fairly unique."

Other redundancies include "advance planning," "close scrutiny," "consensus of opinion," "gathered together" and "past history."

When you're trying to clean up clutter, look for words such as "around" and "up" and "some." They waste space. Also focus on the word "and." When it joins two nouns, verbs or modifiers, ask yourself if you really need both. You probably don't.

"In order to" is also used far too often. Nine times out of 10 that phrase can be replaced simply by "to."

Subject–verb agreement

This is where the "there is" and "there are" example cited earlier comes in. It's critical that singular verbs be used with singular subjects and that plural subjects have plural verbs. When two or more subjects are joined by the coordinating conjunction "and," they take a plural verb. For example, "The managing editor and the senior editor decide three months in advance what the focus of the special section will be." (Because two singular subjects are joined, they form a compound subject—meaning the verb to use is "decide" not "decides.") However, if they are joined by the coordinating conjunction "or," they take a singular verb: "The managing editor or the senior editor decides three months in advance what the focus of the special section will be." (Only one of them decides.)

Tenses

Always make sure that your stories maintain consistent tenses. Far too many novice writers begin in the present tense and then slip into the past. Or they jump back and forth between tenses. This is jarring for the reader and a sign of sloppiness on the part of the writer.

Punctuation

Punctuation is important. In his book, *Reporting and Writing: Basics for the 21st Century*, Christopher Scanlon refers to punctuation marks as "the traffic signals of written language." Although we don't usually think about it, that's exactly how we use punctuation. Commas indicate pauses; exclamation marks express a strong reaction; dashes heighten dramatic effect; parentheses promote understanding; and periods regulate stops and starts.

What about other forms of punctuation? What do they do? Well, the colon (:) is usually used before a list or a quotation—especially if it's a long quotation. Remember that the part of the sentence that comes before the colon must be a complete sentence. For example, "Participating denominations include the following: Baptist, Anglican and Presbyterian," not, "Participating denominations include: Baptist, Anglican and Presbyterian."

The semicolon (;) is halfway between a period and a comma. That is, it indicates a stronger pause than a comma, but a closer connection than a period. It can be used to separate complete sentences that are closely related. The semicolon is also used to separate elements of a series when elements within the series need to be set off by commas. For example, "John Stuart leaves three daughters, Martha (Miller) of Lunenburg, N.S; Melissa (Turner) of Richmond, Ont.; and Anna (Coghill) of Brooks, Alta."

The Writing Process

Writing is easy; all you do is sit staring at a blank sheet of paper until the drops of blood form on your forehead.

– from Writers On Writing, by Gene Fowler

When her three children were young and she had boarders and a husband who worked erratic hours, Hannah Moor used to give herself an hour a day to write. "No matter what I was doing," she said, "I would slide into my desk at nine a.m. and write for an hour—two, if I could manage it. And I always left something unfinished. I didn't want to start the next day by looking at a blank piece of paper, wondering what I'd put down on it."

Of such discipline and tricks is a writer made!

In this chapter we're going to examine some of the subtler aspects of writing—from getting motivated, to confronting writer's block, to finding your voice. Some involve psychology and some involve just plain hard work!

Taking those first steps

Though a good piece of writing may read as if it was written spontaneously, it actually took a lot of planning. You know that research is essential. But before that, seeds need to be planted—seeds that eventually will blossom into stories as a result of researching and writing.

To help keep track of story ideas and to chart events and developing issues, invest in a notebook that is small enough to carry with you. Then don't go anywhere without it. Get into the habit of jotting down story ideas by capturing bits of overheard conversations and observing people and events firsthand.

Gail Reid, managing editor of *Faith Today*, said that's exactly what she does. She particularly likes to note her reactions to news items. "I might read something in the newspaper and a question is raised. So I'll write it down. Writing has always been a way to capture what I'm feeling. So I try to do that every day," she said. "I date everything and often go back to what I've written for column and editorial ideas."

But ideas are only the first step. You'll also need to figure out how to develop your ideas. That takes planning. There is no shortage of time management planners on the market. Buy one. Then use it. It will help you break down your workload (researching, writing, revising and so on) into manageable tasks. This isn't a "To do" list, but is a way of outlining concrete steps that will help you achieve your goal. Who do you need to talk to? What information do you need? Where will you get it—and by when?

Often it helps to surround yourself with words or things that inspire you. Kenn Ward uses this approach. For example, he has the full text of Philippians 2:1–11 posted on a bulletin board by his computer. He also sometimes posts the mission statement of his church or the policies of the magazine. They keep him focused. And they inspire him.

Really getting started (or how to avoid writer's block)

Just when you thought you'd done all the hard stuff, you find yourself up against one of the toughest challenges of all—writer's block. Why does this happen? You've done the research. You've exhausted all your sources. You've got a focus, organized your material into a story structure. Then there's that deadline—staring you in the face. In spite of it all, you can't seem to begin. What's happening?

Sometimes it's easy to fall under the illusion that everything you write must be perfect, must be the final word. In fact, it's only the beginning. No piece is complete without revising/rewriting/changing/altering/correcting, etc.

The best step you can take is to simply get something down—anything. It will get your creative juices flowing and will give you something to work with. You may well end up throwing it all out, but at this stage, that doesn't matter.

Wanting to write is definitely not the same thing as writing. You must discipline yourself to sit at that computer or at the kitchen table with a notebook. And you must begin to lift those facts and images out of your notebook, out of your mind, and into a legible form. Sometimes it feels like one of the hardest things anyone can ever do. It helps, of course, if you have a designated place to write. A place you can call your own, without too many distractions.

However, it doesn't matter how few physical distractions you have if you create mental ones. It's tempting to procrastinate. We all have our little rituals. Pay close attention to yours. Are you getting that extra cup of coffee because it's comforting and stimulates your thinking? Or is it because trotting out to make it provides a rationale for not writing?

Another great excuse for procrastination is the "I-don't-have-enough-time" one. It's easy to fret about the things you don't have control over, as opposed to focusing on those things you do control. It's even easier to complain about time constraints.

Yes, time is always short. All the more reason, then, to use wisely whatever time you have. Initially, use it simply to think about the material you've gathered. Often a percolation process takes place. You've got all those facts and figures and quotations and colourful details swirling around in your head. I'm convinced that something happens to them during sleep. Often they emerge, in waking life, in a pattern you can commit to paper.

This is not to suggest that your subconscious will do all the hard work. The reality is, there's no avoiding the necessary preliminary steps. So check that you have a clear focus, that facts and events are ordered, that you've chosen an appropriate story structure and figured out what kind of effects you want as well as the techniques you'll use to create them.

Finally, trust your inner voice. Your brain may be telling you there are still facts to be gathered and sources to find. If you haven't invested enough time in researching your topic from a variety of angles, this may well be true. But if anything, professionals often over-research. In part, this is because they want to be sure they've covered all the bases. The other part, though, is that continuing the research process is a way of putting off the writing process. If you've done sufficient research, you probably know more about the subject than you think you do. So give your inner voice a chance to express itself. Dive in and start writing.

Writing as a creative endeavour

It often comes as a surprise to even the most seasoned writers that they never know exactly what they're going to say, or how they're going to say it, until it's down on paper.

That has to be one of the most exciting parts of writing. It is also one of the scariest.

Poet and author Kathleen Norris writes in her book, *The Cloister Walk*, that "attentive waiting" is a fair description of the writing process:

> A spark is struck; an event inscribed with a message—*this is important, pay attention*—and a poet scatters a few words like seeds in a notebook. Months or even years later, those words bear fruit. The process requires both discipline and commitment, and its gifts come from both preparedness and grace, or what writers have traditionally called inspiration.

What she is saying is as applicable to non-fiction writing as to fiction writing. And it's no accident that she emphasizes "discipline." In fact, it's not unusual to hear talented people refer to the fact that the harder they work, the more creative they are. (Then again, perhaps, when it comes to this genre, writers can be truly open to the creative only when the steps requiring discipline—researching, interviewing, focusing, story structure, rules of grammar and language—become second nature to them.)

Though writing is definitely a creative endeavour, it can also be an important form of spiritual expression. The two are not mutually exclusive. In fact, the more you develop as a writer, the more you may discover a deepening and enriching of your spiritual life.

Thinking critically

You can't write clearly if you don't think clearly. And thinking requires thought! That may sound redundant, but it isn't. Critical thinking is about how you think and is a necessary first step to becoming a good writer.

One of the characteristics of a critical thinker is the ability to approach issues with an open mind. This doesn't mean you have to discard your own thoughts and feelings about a subject. In fact, it's important to know what you think about issues, where you stand. But having brought your own feelings and attitudes to consciousness, it's essential that you then keep them in check. Don't let them dominate. In that way, you aren't prevented from seeing or hearing another perspective. (This approach dovetails nicely with Lloyd Mackey's definition of conciliatory journalism mentioned in Chapter 3.)

"We traffic in the world of ideas," said Doug Koop. "Our job is to put them out there." And if ideas are to be explored, then it should go without saying that the exploration must be far-reaching and thought provoking.

But thinking critically about issues can be a problem if the leadership of your publication doesn't encourage or welcome independent thought.

"Often there is a fear of confronting divergent or different opinions," said Rick Hiebert, editor of *Testimony*. "I call it the 'fear factor.' Perhaps the fear is that if people disagree, then they'll leave the church. But the church is a microcosm of Canada. There is genuine pluralism in it and I want to reflect that, I want to be creative. I want to examine belief. I want to see a broad spectrum of thought in my magazine."

It's unfortunate when this perspective is interpreted as disloyalty or a challenge to the faith. Hiebert, for example, said he is strong in his faith: "I'm a believer. I'm very committed to the tenets of our faith, to belief in Jesus Christ. In fact, everything I do comes from my relationship with Christ. And to me, this should be reflected in the work that I do."

Hiebert does this by approaching ideas and issues critically and by encouraging others to do the same. In fact, anyone serious about personal growth *must* be able to ask questions—and then not be afraid of hearing the answers. Far too many people are only too happy to provide simple answers to tough questions. However, thoughtful Christian publications attempt to confront tough issues by grappling with them. Part of this is being willing to struggle with understanding alternative perspectives.

I once came across an article that outlined eight characteristics of critical thinking. Not surprisingly, the first one was asking questions. The others included defining a problem, examining evidence, analyzing assumptions and biases, avoiding emotional reasoning, avoiding oversimplification, considering other interpretations and, finally, tolerating ambiguity.

Though these are admirable characteristics for anyone to have, they are particularly important for writers. Though the word isn't generally welcome in religious circles, I like to think of critical thinkers as "skeptical." I don't mean this in the traditional sense of doubting the truth of religion. I mean being wary of those who are so certain of themselves and their views that they attempt to impose them on others. These kinds of people often actively work to exclude the possibility of alternate perspectives being aired.

To me, skepticism is another way to describe coming to issues with an open mind.

Skepticism is not the same as cynicism. I consider skepticism to be a virtue in professional journalists because it involves an inquiring approach, an openness to hearing people out, to being reflective in the search for truth. Cynicism, on the other hand, is characterized by doubting, even sneering, at the motives of others. It's about thinking you know the answer before you ask the question. It's about never allowing for surprise or discovery. Cynicism is the enemy of writing in the service of your readers.

If you find yourself feeling cynical about the people or the issues you cover, then it's time to rethink what you are doing with your life. At the very least, search your soul to find the source of it. Ask for help. Or leave the job altogether. There is no place in this line of work for cynicism. Your words will be poison, and you will not be able to do justice to your readers.

Knowing yourself

A large part of writing for the Christian press involves studying the work and actions of others. However, this shouldn't be used as an excuse for avoiding self-knowledge, self-awareness. In fact, knowing yourself is an important part of being both a critical thinker and a good writer. This is because writing—good writing—comes from the heart. Through the act of writing you share something of who you are, where you're coming from and how you view the world.

I'm not referring to writing in the first person. Nor am I referring to writing commentary. Instead, I'm referring to the way you use words, the route you chart for readers to follow— no matter what form your writing takes. Kathleen Norris writes, "The hard work of writing has taught me that in matters of the heart, such as writing, or faith, there is no right or wrong way to do it, but only the way of your life."

So, consciously strive for self-awareness, for insight into what motivates you and where your strengths and weaknesses lie. For some this involves prayer and meditation, reading widely, thinking critically, keeping a journal and participating in a Bible study group.

At the same time, knowing yourself means keeping your own biases and perspectives in the background when others are the subject. The better you know yourself, the better able you will be to treat the views of others fairly. Become aware of those occasions when your views may stand in the way of the expression of the views of others.

Joe Sinasac, editor of *The Catholic Register*, said he was asked in his first journalism class why he wanted to be a journalist. "I said, 'I want to change the world.' I think Catholics become either priests or journalists for the same reason; they love to be on the soap box. They want to reveal truth to others. That's what drew me to journalism."

But it was a growing sense of self-awareness that caused Sinasac to move from secular, or mainstream, journalism to the Christian press. "In the secular world, I couldn't be explicit," he said. "I could live [faith], but I couldn't talk it. Here, I can express myself openly in the context of my faith."

And as David Harris, editor of the *Presbyterian Record*, puts it, "We bring *all* that we are to our writing—including our faith." Being aware of "all that you are" can help you grow, not just personally, but professionally, in your writing and in the service of your readers.

Finding your voice

Hannah Moor trained to go to the mission field. That's where she felt she could make a real contribution, where she could live her Christian beliefs. But just before departing, poor health thwarted that dream. It was a shock. There were more to come—riding the rough seas of harsh economic times, for one. "But writing," she said, "was something that just seemed to be in me." So she wrote verse—a lot of it. However, no one wanted to buy verse. Then one day a friend suggested she write a short story.

"I thought I couldn't do it, and so I sat down to prove to her that I couldn't," she said. "But much to my surprise, I actually wrote a saleable story. In fact, I wrote a number of them. Then I started to get rejections and I had to learn what writing was all about."

Moor enrolled in writing courses, which were useful. But one rejection, in particular, helped her find her way. It came from an American publishing company called the Union

Gospel Press. "Their policy was to have three readers assess a work," she said. "Each one would make comments on a separate sheet of paper, and those comments would be passed on to the next person until a final decision was made. But when you got your story back, you didn't see any of the comments. You just got accepted or rejected."

"One time," she continued, "one of the reader's slip of paper had been inadvertently left inside my story. I'll never forget it. It said, 'Not written in the true Hannah Moor style.' It made me wonder what my style was. So I went back and looked through everything I'd written and tried to see how they were structured and what made them my 'style.'"

Another word for "style" is "voice"—the writer's voice. "Voice" is essentially the presence of a style that characterizes a writer. It means that you write in such a way that readers see the world through your eyes. It means bringing life to details. Voice isn't something you can manufacture at will or grab out of thin air. Nor does it mean that you must write in the first person. In fact, as noted above, a writer's voice usually comes out subconsciously and is very much present when writing in the third person.

Does "voice" mean something different when writing journalistically, as opposed to writing fiction? Not necessarily. One of the functions of "voice" is to give readers a role in the article. If you've adopted the voice of the journalist, you're asking them to share your approach—to see the issue or event or people you're writing about through the lens of someone seeking to uncover the meaning of the facts you uncover.

Christopher Scanlon gives writing workshops through the Poynter Institute. He's also written a book on reporting and writing. In it, he says that the way to find your voice is "to write, of course, but also to use your powers of speech and hearing to discover your voice by listening and tuning the words until they say what you want them to say in just the way you want them to say it. Read your words aloud.... If the sound of your story puts you to sleep, imagine how the reader will respond."

Writing affects others

Words have the power to change a human heart. So writers have a lot of power—and a lot of responsibility. But unless people tell you, you have no way of knowing what kind of effect your stories have on others. However, it's safe to say that well researched stories, written with clarity and style about a subject that people care about, are going to affect them. Such stories will inform and, hopefully, provoke, enlighten and inspire.

Good, strong writing is one of the keys. Harold Jantz, founding editor of *Christian Week*, said his goal in all the stories he wrote and edited was to communicate "the redemption and transformation of people within our world. Even though we sometimes had heavy controversies and bad stories to tell, I always maintained that we represented a 'third voice' within the denomination. We were the third partner there—not the mouthpiece of the church leadership—but as a means to communicate between church leaders and those who were within the church. I tried to give those voices as much legitimacy as those who were leaders."

What Jantz is talking about, of course, is empowerment. It's a thread that runs through the conversations of all the Christian press editors I talked to. They understand the importance of provoking thought, of providing readers with insights into their faith and how issues affect their lives and intersect with others. Strong writers, telling powerful stories, move people.

"I see so much hope," said Ted Schmidt, editor of *Catholic New Times*. "People send us money to keep us alive. In some small way, what they're doing is part of a broader community of saints around the world fighting the good fight against globalization, against poverty."

As a writer for the Christian press, you occupy a position of privilege—a soapbox from which to present your work. This gives you power. Both the privilege and the power come with enormous responsibilities to act in the public interest. Never lose sight of your mission to serve the community you represent. Judge your work in that context.

Writing as therapy

Gail Reid didn't intend to be a writer. Her training was in psychiatric social work, but after a burnout she decided she needed both help and a change in direction. The Christian psychiatrist she met with suggested she try writing. It was exactly what she needed.

"It gave me the permission to write about issues and things in my life, about people I met," said Reid. It meant that when she felt angry or upset or frightened, she could use words to express her feelings, as well as her passions. As she put it, "When the words capture it, then I can let it go. It's therapeutic."

Interestingly, although she started to write for a personal reason, Reid was surprised to discover that when she shared what she'd written with others, they reacted positively. "They said that I'd articulated what they couldn't put into words," she said.

This is what every writer strives for. Good writing explores the human condition and, in the process, it hopefully touches a nerve. The initial motivation behind putting words to paper may be to help oneself. But the outcome may be that others are helped as well. Hannah Moor, for example, said that when she and her family went through some tough economic times, it was good to be able to put it on paper. "I got it out of my system," she said. "And I knew that I wasn't alone. Many people were really suffering and hurting. I felt that if I could just get something in writing that they could read, then maybe it could help."

Writing is also informed by the subconscious, and it often involves making the subconscious conscious. The impact on you, the writer, can be like an unburdening—a thoroughly therapeutic and liberating experience that involves considerable trust in your inner voice. See it as a resource you can tap.

Writing changes you

If writing for you is a "holy calling," as Doug Koop put it, then this means it's certainly more than a job, more than a way of meeting expenses. Anyone I've ever met from the Christian press has maintained that their work contributes both to their development in, and understanding of, their faith.

Ian Adnams, editor of *Canadian Lutheran*, said he thinks the nature of the subject matter moves writers in mysterious ways. "The unique thing about covering religion is that it will have an impact on you. It will affect you," he said. "This can be scary for secular journalists covering religion because there is an unquantifiable element—something happens—when they're covering faith. And they can't understand or explain it."

Certainly the act of covering diverse views has an effect. "I've grown because I've been exposed to a lot of people and to their ideas," said Kenn Ward, former editor of *The Canada Lutheran*. "This work has helped me understand that people who don't agree with me on the basis of Scripture aren't wrong, but they're coming at things from a different way. So I've learned to read and to listen carefully to what others are saying."

In fact, Ward said it's been a revelation to discover that being open to differences, by airing them and discussing them in a spirit of respect, has allowed him to become friends with critics, with people with whom he might originally have thought he shared little common ground.

Joe Sinasac said he treasures the ways in which his work has brought him into contact with incredibly holy people— "not pious, but people who are really in touch with our hurts and the Lord, and people who can instill the love of God in others. They inspire me," he said.

But the opposite has also happened. There have been times, Sinasac said, when he's been disillusioned by the behaviour of people whom he previously respected. "These are challenges to your faith," he said. "But I've definitely matured spiritually. In my late teens I saw spirituality as going to retreats and looking for spiritual highs. Now I've come to understand that I can't live without faith, without Christianity. I hope that helps me rise above all the evil I see in the world, and even above my own faults."

Though your faith may provide a framework for how you live your life, it certainly doesn't mean that the answers to every issue or obstacle are always obvious. For columnists, grappling to find what they think about an issue and how it relates to their faith, this work can be both challenging and profound.

Muriel Duncan, editor of *The United Church Observer*, said that the discipline of writing a column has taken her "into places I might not normally go. I've had to stretch myself. Sometimes I don't have an opinion about an issue, but I have to go into it and see not only why it's important, but ask myself, 'Is this what I believe?'" She said it's also allowed her to feel comfortable with ambiguity.

Your work gives you the opportunity to test your own ideas and preconceptions in the real world you cover and against the perspective of others you meet and report on. In the process, your views will change and mature. Possibilities for growth in this profession are as great as your readiness to be open to new truths.

The intellectual stimulation may be as basic as learning more about the history and doctrines of one's faith. "It's been good for me to learn about the nuances, and the things that make me Lutheran," said Adnams. "Getting to understand my faith better is a wonderful learning experience."

Added Marianne Meed Ward: "When I first joined *Faith Today*, I had no idea of the different types of denominations and where they came from. It opened my eyes to all the kindred spirits out there. There were many I would have disagreed with, but it was energizing to find thoughtful people who struggled with issues of faith and were part of that community. In fact, it kept me in the institutional fold because I saw so many people I liked and respected within it."

Catholic Missions in Canada features stories from 683 missionaries and the people they serve in some of the poorest and most remote parts of Canada. (In fact, the eight mission dioceses in the north straddle two-thirds of the land mass of Canada.) Editor Patria Rivera said she is often moved by the vision of these missionaries and by the joy and meaning they find in their faith. "Today, in a society that puts emphasis on the temporal, what is current and what is cool, perhaps *Catholic Missions in Canada* magazine, and others like it, offer a safe harbour for souls starving for true meaning," she said.

Rivera's point is underlined in the writing of Oblate Father Brian Ballard, a missionary priest. He wrote of his experiences going into remote areas.

> We waited for three days for the snow to settle [on the frozen lake] so we could have a proper runway. And we tried to get the plane off the ice each time and could not succeed. Or in the summer we traveled 12 hours on rough roads to a mission. But this is just physical hardship.

163

The more difficult part is the ache, or the yearning, to be able to touch people's hearts in an age when the experience and presence of faith is getting farther and farther away from the young people's immediate reality because their elders have passed on and are no longer there to guide them in their faith journey. Yet, the hallmark of our presence here is the wonderful joy that we get being with the people. There's no other place I'd like to be.

Father Brian Ballard died on Aug. 20, 2001, when his plane crashed in the Hugh Allan Basin area in British Columbia.

7 Ethics

The person featured in the story seemed just too good to be true. Encapsulating all the characteristics necessary to illustrate the focus of the story, the character came complete with name and identity. The problem was, the person *was* too good to be true.

Rick Hiebert, who had commissioned and edited the feature story for the *Testimony*, said there was something about that person that bothered him. But he trusted his writer. It was only later, when Hiebert pressed him, that he discovered the character was a composite. The writer had amalgamated the characteristics of a number of actual people and created a new one. The name and identity he had given this new person were fictional. And he had revealed none of this to readers.

The writer had crossed an ethical line. "I was disgusted," said Hiebert. "I felt that my trust was betrayed. Now I am very, very careful."

That writer might have created a composite for what he felt were the right reasons; no doubt he wanted to protect both the privacy and identity of his sources, and he probably thought such a perfect illustration would entice people to read an important story. However understandable the rationale, what he did was wrong. He crossed an ethical line. He led readers to believe that fiction was fact. Though he might have been able to make a case for giving his source a pseudonym, readers should have been told that he'd done so and been given the reason why.

Unfortunately, this sort of thing does happen (and probably, more often than not, with no malicious intent). That's the reason for this chapter. At first glance, it might seem peculiar to include a chapter on ethics for Christian writers. After all, attempting to live with integrity on a daily basis is an important part of what it is to be a practicing Christian.

But becoming a writer doesn't come with a "How to" manual. The secular press has struggled for decades with the kinds of ethical behaviour the public has a right to expect from its professional journalists. Gail Reid of *Faith Today* said Christian writers and editors, above all, must adhere to the highest professional standards. "We need to not only be faithful to the Creator," she said, "but we must be in alignment with ethics that can be brought to light."

"Ethics" is not the same as "morals," although moral choices are often involved. Ethics is really a set of principles that guide conduct. "Doing the right thing" is another way of putting it. Though some of the situations we're going to examine in this chapter are black and white, many aren't. Often you will find yourself in a situation in which your choices come in various tones of grey. Those represent the toughest decisions. They are also the ones that take place behind the scenes. Readers will never know what the writer grappled with long before the story saw the light of day. "There are many times when I've chosen to do something, and no one knows," said Reid. "But God knows."

In this chapter, we'll examine some of the situations that

writers and editors might find themselves in—situations that require judgment, thought and, above all, the ability to make sound ethical decisions. We'll also explore a guide that can be used to help you make good decisions.

The use and abuse of quotations

Quotations are critical to good stories. A good quotation can take the reader immediately to the heart of a story. It can help focus your story, provide characterization and provide essential facts. But if you're using a quotation, it must be accurate and must reflect the context of the discussion in which it took place. (Having said that, most editors agree that altering a quotation to correct egregious grammar or to avoid dialect that isn't essential to the story is not unethical.)

Your job is to impart meaning in as clear and concise a way as possible. That's why changing a quotation that contains bad grammar is often considered acceptable. However, there is no consensus. Certainly most people think that if there are quotation marks around a quotation, then what they are reading are the exact words that someone spoke. Often, it's just as easy to write around the bad grammar. You can paraphrase what the person said, or just use a fragment of the quotation. Then again, you can use ellipses. Ellipses are the three little dots you might come across in news stories (...). They tell readers that one or more words have been omitted from the quotation they are reading.

What if you want to use a quotation from someone you haven't interviewed, but you saw the person quoted in your daily newspaper? First, try to arrange for your own interview. If that isn't possible, use the quotation—but only if you attribute it. For example, you might write: "Last month, His Eminence Aloysius Cardinal Ambrozic told the *Montreal Gazette....*"

One of the managing editors I worked under at the *Toronto Star* was adamant that all interviews be done in person if at all possible. If not, readers needed to be told. So it was common for a story to read, "In a telephone interview, John Doe said...." To him, readers had a right to know how the information was gathered as he believed it could have an impact on the quality of the material.

Finally, remember that even a direct quotation isn't "true" if it's taken out of context. Context is everything. So don't just get the quotation right, but use it appropriately,

Dealing with sources

Your sources should be treated with scrupulous honesty. This means identifying yourself to people as a reporter/writer with a particular publication, explaining why you want to talk to them and what you want to talk to them about. Then making clear that you intend to quote them in a subsequent article.

Joe Sinasac, editor of the *Catholic Register*, said he tries to impress upon his writers "the need to treat sources not as raw material but as human beings. This means treating them with dignity and respect. It also means making sure they know that what they're saying is 'on the record.' People often have to be told what is meant by that because they don't automatically know. Often, they think you're just asking advice. Then they're surprised when you quote them."

People need to be given the ground rules. Or, perhaps to put it more realistically, ground rules need to be negotiated up front and honestly. This means reaching an understanding about whether something is on the record (the information can be used) or off the record (nothing the person told you can be used in the story). However, should off-the-record information be confirmed by an independent source, then you can use it.

Anonymous sources

You should also reach an understanding about whether the material is for attribution or not. "Attribution" is part of being on the record. It means you tell readers where the information came from—the name and title of your source. Normally, once you've identified yourself as a reporter with such and such publication, you can assume that people understand that they might be quoted. However, as Sinasac pointed out, that isn't necessarily the case—especially with people who don't have a lot of experience with the media.

When you agree that someone will give you material that is "not for attribution," it means that you can use the information, but you can't say in your story where you got the information from. When you promise "not for attribution," you're guaranteeing your source that no one will be able to identify him or her by the way in which you use the information. "Not for attribution" is generally used for obtaining background information about an issue, event or person.

There has been a distressing increase in the use of unattributed information. Sources who refuse to be identified may be seeking to manipulate media outlets to their own advantage by remaining anonymous. Information that can't be attributed deserves a skeptical response from both journalists and readers. Relying on such sources too much will hurt your credibility.

There may be situations in which you will promise not to identify a source in your story. However, this should be done in rare instances only. If you regularly offer readers stories with anonymous sources, they will rightly wonder where the line lies between fact and fiction. Are these people real, or are they a figment of your imagination? If someone could be hurt by being named in your story, then you'll have to think very hard about your choices. There is the legal aspect (outlined in Chapter 8). But there is also the ethical one. You will need to

169

weigh that person's need for privacy against your readership's right to know.

If you do promise anonymity, you must tell your source that you can promise anonymity on one condition only: that your editor will be informed of the person's name and identity. Your editor *must* know that the sources in your story are genuine and *must* have contact information if further verification is required.

Rich Hiebert said he is now very, very careful about checking the validity of sources in the stories that run in his magazine. This is especially important, he said, given that his denomination places such an emphasis on healing. "People are so pleased when a miracle occurs," he said. "But I ask for confirmation from a doctor who can at least attest that something has happened. And I want to know who the pastor is. I want to hear that the person [who was healed] is respectable. I insist on that. It is one of my safeguards. It's time-consuming, but I tell writers, 'This is what I need from you.' If there are any questions, then that's my first line of defence. Real names, real people, and confirmation of what happened."

Then there are the stories in which an unnamed source is used to make a telling comment against someone else or on a controversial issue. Unfortunately, it's becoming increasingly common to see anonymous sources quoted in mainstream newspaper stories to malign or cast aspersions on public figures. This is unacceptable. There may be a rare occasion in which "a source within the department" is quoted because that information is essential to exposing a larger picture. But for the most part, it should be avoided.

Gifts

You probably won't find yourself in many situations in which someone you're writing about passes you a gift. This can far too easily be interpreted as a form of bribery, a fact that's as obvious to sources as it is to journalists. It is a clear case of conflict of interest. But it continues to be a problem in subtler forms—accepting favours or getting special treatment.

The School of Journalism's Code of Ethics at Carleton University encourages students to use common sense. A cup of coffee, for example, clearly isn't a gift. The important thing is to refuse to accept special treatment or favours from sources and to avoid even the appearance of doing so.

Conflict of interest

It should go without saying that you mustn't write about something you're specifically involved in. Your readers must be able to trust your work; they mustn't read a story and then be left wondering whether you had a personal stake in its outcome.

A corollary of that is not interviewing friends or family members for stories—not, that is, unless you make the relationship clear to your readers. If you don't make this clear, and it later comes out, your professionalism will be called into question. People will wonder how much balance you can bring to a story if you are personally close to a source.

However, having no conflict of interest in a story is not good enough. You must also work hard to avoid the *appearance* of a conflict of interest. That means not putting yourself in a situation in which your work or your motives could be misconstrued as a conflict of interest.

Vetting copy

Another word for "vetting" is editing. That's what happens after a story is written and submitted to an editor. The editor's job is to ensure that the story has integrity, that sources are legitimate, that the story is balanced and fair, that all the bases are covered (background, context, analysis, if applicable) and that it reads well. If anything falls short, the editor will ask the writer to go back to the drawing board and make changes.

The fact that this job is for the editor—and for the editor *alone*—is often not particularly well understood by people within religious circles. Editors are professionals. Presumably they have their jobs because of their training, because of their understanding of the nuances of the faith and because of their commitment to communicating through stories and pictures the mission statement of the publication.

David Harris of the *Presbyterian Record* noted that "in the religious press, there's as much naïveté about ethics in journalism as there is lack of awareness of religious nuances in the secular press. People [from the religious community] have asked to see a story before it runs. I say, 'No.' But then they will say, 'What if there are mistakes in it?' I tell them that if I have any doubts, I'll ask. But it's our responsibility as professionals to get it right. And it's a job we take very seriously because we know the impact of getting something wrong."

There are two ways in which the naïveté Harris refers to expresses itself. One is when people in leadership positions in the church want to see stories in advance of their publication. The other is when sources ask to read a story in advance of its publication. Both situations have to be one of the most frustrating aspects of the job for editors, and they can create unnecessary problems for novice writers.

Kenn Ward, for example, said someone once came to him with a story idea about writing a profile on a man who, despite living with a terrible disease, was doing terrific work in the church. Ward gave the writer the go-ahead. After finishing the story—and before submitting it to Ward—the writer showed the story to the man being profiled. He'd asked to see it and it apparently it hadn't occurred to the writer that this might be an unprofessional, even an unethical, thing to do.

The man read the story and, not surprisingly, made changes in the copy. (As Gail Reid noted, "Nobody *ever* likes the way that they're quoted.") However, in this instance, the man not only changed his quotations, but by the time Ward got the story all references to his disease had been eliminated. "Then it wasn't a story," said Ward. "There are a lot of people doing wonderful work in the church. What made this a story was that he did such wonderful work while living with a disease."

Here's something to think about—something that might help you remember why showing a pre-publication copy of your story to *anyone* who played *any* role in it is a bad idea: your readers and your editor need to be able to trust you. Your editor needs to be able to trust that your story represents your best effort to provide fairness, balance and accuracy. Your story must reflect your journalistic choices, not the personal agenda of your sources. You cannot afford to be beholden to anyone other than your organization's readers and your professional ethics. If your editor or your readers have reason to doubt your professionalism, then you will lose their trust—trust that could take years to earn back, if you ever can.

Muriel Duncan said she simply tells people who want to read her stories in advance of publication that they're going to have to trust her. "And then I have to [justify] that trust."

The other kind of "vetting" situation occurs when church authorities want to read stories in advance. Ward said that sometimes happens, usually with someone who was interviewed for the story. He tells them he's happy to check specific quotations for accuracy with them. But he won't show them an entire story. "They need to remember that the magazine isn't a mouthpiece of the church," he said. "This is critical. Sometimes in the short run, it may feel easier to sacrifice that right [of professional independence], but in the long run, it definitely isn't. People—readers—need to be able to trust us."

Here's another way to look at it: just imagine how you'd feel if you learned that every political story you read in your daily newspaper or heard on your radio or saw on your nightly television newscast had been submitted to the prime minister's office before being published or broadcast? How could you trust that news outlet? How could you trust the writers? Bottom line is, you couldn't. You'd have good reason to think you were being fed propaganda, not news and current affairs. Don't put yourself in an analogous situation.

Harold Jantz said he learned early on how important it is to insist on editorial independence. "There were a few times when people in leadership were uncomfortable," he said. "At one point I was told to submit my material to a committee to be vetted. I said I wouldn't do that and that I wouldn't continue in the job if they insisted. So they decided not to ask for that. I had to be firm. However," he added, "I wasn't alone. I had strong support from others."

Jantz said one of his biggest concerns came from people who would try "to shut us down before we had a chance to publish. They'd try to take legal action. It's a form of intimidation and prevents the truth from coming out. But I was told that the best defence is the truth and the ability to provide evidence. And sure enough, when people realize you won't be intimidated, they withdraw."

Plagiarism

Plagiarism is something you probably learned about in school. It is when you take someone else's words or ideas and attempt to pass them off as your own. Unfortunately, because of technology, it's easier than ever to commit this literary crime. The Internet is readily accessible and it's easy to cut and paste things. You might put them into a file and end up using them as your own—not because of a conscious intent to mislead, but because you got sloppy, or time was tight, and you didn't properly label your notes.

A good way to avoid plagiarism is to give credit where credit is due. Always attribute information, or ideas, to their source. And keep good notes. Source them and be prepared to point others to the materials if they want to do any further investigation.

Fabrication

Fabricating material is one of the worst professional sins you can commit. It's when you intentionally invent information, quotations, data or sources. It violates one of the most sacred rules of journalism: Don't invent content. You should strive to be inventive in terms of presentation and writing style, but never in terms of substance.

Accuracy

As outlined in previous chapters, good writing takes readers to the places you've been, to the people you've talked to. But there will also be times when you'll want to reconstruct an event, a scenario that you didn't witness yourself. How can you ensure accuracy? How can you ensure that, in recreating an event, you are reporting truthfully and ethically?

Bob Steele, ethics director at The Poynter Institute, and Christopher Scanlon, author of *Reporting and Writing: Basics for the 21st century*, have compiled a checklist of questions to help you make good ethical decisions. They include

❏ How do I know that what I have presented really happened the way I say it did?

❑ Who says it's true?

❑ How many sources have I based my reconstruction on?

❑ Did I get independent verification from other sources—sources I have reason to be confident of?

❑ Am I willing, and able, to fully disclose and explain my method of reconstruction to my editor, to my readers?

Reconstruction can be a dramatic way to engage readers and convey reality, but it requires painstaking research and corroboration to be journalistically and ethically sound.

Photographs

Examining the ethical aspect of how photographs are used in journalism could constitute a book in itself. Though we can't explore it in depth here, it is worth raising because most Christian publications use photos to accompany stories. Understanding that the use of photos with stories raises ethical issues of its own is important.

Kenn Ward said his eyes were opened when he took a photo editing course at *The Winnipeg Sun*. He said discussion centred around such topics as, When is it ethical to take photographs? as well as, How should photographs be used? In a day and age in which technology makes it possible to alter all kinds of images with the flick of a key, Ward said he learned the importance of acting with caution.

"If you doctor a photograph at all, then you must label it a photo illustration," he said. "Say you wanted to move someone out of the middle of a photograph. That's fine, as long as you label it a "photo illustration." But if you move the person and let it run as a straight photograph, then readers won't be able to trust you. They'd have reason to think that if you manipulated that, then perhaps you're manipulating other things, as well."

Similarly, photographs that are used for emotional value or that depict persons unrelated to the story must be true to the context and be properly identified. They should not be used to exaggerate or to misrepresent. Finally, some photographs can come across as exploitative if they invade private space or portray gratuitous emotion.

Context and other considerations

Context

Muriel Duncan of *The United Church Observer* said she once covered a meeting in which the assembled officials were called to make a prayer of repentance as a result of a decision they'd made some time earlier. They debated and discussed it and then, in the end, decided they weren't yet ready. They voted against offering the prayer.

"There I was, sitting at the back of the room, having a story that would say they'd refused to pray," said Duncan. "It was clearly something they'd like not to be in the story."

In the hands of an unscrupulous reporter, such a story would be front-page news, coupled with a damning headline. In the hands of a reporter whose first allegiance was to church authorities, as opposed to the readership, the result of the vote might have been expunged. Both would have been unethical.

Duncan chose professionalism. She reported what happened, but she didn't play it out of proportion. Nor did she make it appear to be something other than what it was. It wasn't that church officials *refused* to offer a prayer of repentance, but that they felt they weren't ready to do it right then. Duncan provided readers with a true and full account of what happened. In other words, she described the discussion. She put the vote in context. Readers could then form their own opinions about the outcome.

Providing context to quotations and events is a necessary requirement of good reporting and writing. Only by providing context can you be fair and accurate to the meaning of your story. Without context, readers can't fully grasp how or why something happened. Without context, you are failing to be fully accurate in your reporting. You are also failing to act ethically.

Objectivity

Though objectivity is often touted as a prerequisite of ethical journalism, David Harris puts paid to the notion of pure objectivity. "I'm the son of an Anglican priest, and a baptized, practicing Christian," he said. "I've had nine years of university and have worked for 15 years in journalism—two-thirds in the secular and one-third in the religious. I'm also a white male in my 40s, living and working in Canada All those things are there. I can't bifurcate myself."

Every time Harris writes or edits a story he brings those attributes to his work. But he also strives for self-awareness, for recognizing and acknowledging what he brings, so it doesn't unduly colour what he sees, hears, writes or edits. As he puts it, "It's realizing, when you write, what your prejudices are and making sure they don't unduly influence you."

To say that true objectivity doesn't exist, however, doesn't mean that it isn't a worthy ideal. When a journalist strives for objectivity, she isn't pretending to be free of prejudice. But she is committing herself to the pursuit of accuracy and the search for facts that point to truth.

Maintaining a respect for the basics is another good way to keep on the straight and narrow. This means answering the five Ws and H in all your stories, and attributing material to authoritative sources. It also means being open to your own prejudices and the assumptions you bring to issues and events. Finally, it means bringing a healthy dose of skepticism to your stories. This doesn't mean suspecting that every source is trying to pull the wool over your eyes. But it does mean checking and double-checking so that accuracy becomes a hallmark of your writing.

Story selection

There could be an ethical component to your choice of which stories to cover. Are you choosing only stories that reinforce or fit your way of thinking? Are you intentionally choosing certain stories to prove a point? Or are you selecting stories that will provide important content for your readers and that reflect their priorities and interests?

Source selection

It is unethical to look only for sources that agree with you. Diversity of opinion and perspective is important if readers are to get fair and balanced stories.

Fact selection and arrangement

The only way a story can be balanced is if the facts you've compiled come from equally authoritative sources. If you devote your lead and the next 12 paragraphs to one perspective, and throw in an opposing perspective only at the end, you're failing in your ethical responsibility to present the facts in a balanced manner.

Language selection

Language can be highly prejudicial. A very different effect is created for readers if you write "she admitted" or "he claimed," rather than "he or she said." And, when describing people, be careful that you don't move from reporting to editorializing. The shift can be almost imperceptible. However, the effect is not.

Codes of ethics

A journalistic code of ethics is simply a written set of guidelines that describe what kind of behaviour is expected of, and appropriate to, reporters and editors. In 1981, the Canadian Church Press adopted a code of ethics (http://www.canadianchurchpress.com/sections/code-ofethics.shtml). It stresses accuracy and professional responsibility as well as the need to work cooperatively and in mutual respect with other Christians. Today most mainstream media outlets have a code of ethics.

Interestingly, although there are many codes in existence, there is no universal code of ethics for journalists. No matter what the media outlet, though, some principles are common to them all. There's the idea that journalists have a responsibility to serve the public and that they shouldn't use their positions for private profit. There's the idea that news reports should be fair and balanced and accurate, that various sides of a dispute should have their say and that if an error is made, it be corrected immediately. These ideas were first developed by the late Lou Hodges of Washington and Lee University. He raised the issue of media ethics in his 1976 book, *The Messenger's Motives*.

A guide to ethical decision-making

Lou Hodges, an ordained Methodist minister, earned his doctorate in Christian thought, with a special emphasis in ethics. He argued that every professional judgment made by journalists contains a moral component. Thanks to him and his work, secular journalists now include ethics as a central point of discussion when examining their work.

Hodges argued that journalists should ask themselves the following questions when grappling with an ethical issue.

They are

- ❏ What are the issues?
- ❏ What are the relevant facts?
- ❏ What are the possible courses of action?
- ❏ What are the likely consequences of those actions?
- ❏ Which course of action should I take?

These are good questions and can help you make good ethical decisions. However, you will often find that answering those questions as honestly as possible doesn't always give you a clear answer. Or you may find that it provides you with an answer that runs against the tide of conventional thinking in secular journalism.

For example, Gail Reid said that once, during an interview, a source made a startling revelation. "He told me something he shouldn't have," she said. "At Ryerson, where I studied, they'd say that what he said was 'truth,' was 'cutting edge.' But I felt I was facing an ethical situation. I felt that what he told me was something he would have been embarrassed to have in print. So I made the Christian decision not to print it."

As she said, others in her situation might have played it very differently. They might have assumed that this person knowingly made the revelatory comments and that he would have to bear the consequences. They might even argue that, by telling it to a writer, he wanted that information to come out and that she had no right to rob him of that decision. Which is right? In fact, is there a "right" decision? There is rarely a right or a wrong in these things and it often does come down to a personal choice.

However, you should never jump to making that choice. Carefully consider all of the complexities of the situation. Ask yourself the hard questions and answer them as truthfully as possible. Discuss the situation with your editor or with someone whose judgment you trust. Recognize and admit that these situations require rigorous thought. And then make sure the decision is one you can live with.

The Society of Professional Journalists in the U.S. has adopted a code of ethics. It considers the essentials of ethical reporting and writing to be seeking truth and reporting it, minimizing harm, acting independently and being accountable. You can find a full description of this code on the Internet (https://www.spj.org/ethics_code.asp).

A Journalist's Moral Framework

- ❑ Loyalty to the facts. "Devotion to fact, to truth, is a necessary moral demand." (John Dewey)
- ❑ An involvement in the affairs of men and women that requires compassion, accuracy and fairness.
- ❑ The ability to distance one's self from experience to generate understanding.
- ❑ Detached curiosity. An exploratory attitude toward events and ideas. Being bound by evidence and reasonable deductions.
- ❑ A reverence for shared values, rules, codes, laws and arrangements that give a sense of community.
- ❑ Faith in experience when intelligently used as a means of disclosing some truths.
- ❑ An avoidance of valueless objectivity—an attitude of not caring, passivity and non-attachment.
- ❑ A willingness to hold belief in suspense—to doubt until evidence is obtained, to go where the evidence points instead of putting first a personally preferred conclusion,

to hold ideas in solution and use them as hypotheses instead of dogmas to be asserted.

❏ An awareness of our limitations and responsibilities. A firm understanding of the line between fact and fiction.

❏ A belief in the methods of journalism—the conviction that this method will lead to some kind of truth worth sharing.

❏ A moral vision of the future. Without a moral vision, the compulsion may be power, profit and place in society.

❏ An understanding that our words have consequences and that we have some responsibility for the consequences.

❏ A willingness to be active rather than reactive. Go to the community to help define the issues—don't overly depend on official, usually powerful, sources.

Paraphrased from Melvin Mencher's moral framework for journalists, as outlined in his book *News Reporting and Writing*.

The Law Giveth and the Law Taketh Away

—Klaus Pohle

One of the most important cornerstones of any democracy is freedom of speech and of the press. Free speech generally allows us to receive information and, in turn, impart information to others. It allows us to discuss, debate and argue passionately about the great—and small—issues of the day without fear of censorship. Simply put, it ensures that our opinions and ideas will not get us into trouble with the authorities even if they challenge conventional wisdom or the accepted orthodoxy of the day—or democracy itself. No democracy can survive for very long—or is even entitled to call itself a democracy—without a well-developed system of free speech.

It is for that reason that the English poet, John Milton, as far back as 1642, famously asked for "the liberty to know, to utter, and argue freely according to conscience, above all liberties."[1] Taking up that challenge in more modern times, free speech scholars such as the American Thomas Emerson iden-

---

[1] John Milton, *Areopagitica* (1644).

tified four functions, or utilities, served by a system of free expression: individual self-fulfillment, search for truth, self-governance or participation in governmental decision making, and promoting stability.[2] Ultimately, free speech and a free press are supposed to enable an enlightened citizenry to make informed democratic decisions.

A free press is part and parcel of such a system and is similarly crucial to survival of democracy. It may be a cliché to say so, but a robust press that is able to present information without fear of legal repercussions, that is able to question and challenge, is still the best protection against overbearing and intrusive governments as well as others in society who would seek to oppress others.

It is for that reason that most liberal democracies, Canada included, have enshrined freedom of expression as a constitutionally guaranteed right. In Canada, this freedom was first enshrined in the constitution in the 1982 *Charter of Rights and Freedoms*.[3] Section 2 guarantees certain fundamental freedoms including "freedom of conscience and religion," and "freedom of thought, belief, opinion and expression, including freedom of the press and other media of communication...." The *Charter* also guarantees such rights as presumption of innocence, a fair and public trial, and equality before the law.

Prior to 1982 there was no constitutional protection of such rights in Canada. In those days civil liberties were not a right but a privilege that could be limited or even taken away by Parliament or a legislature at any time as long as the proper level of government enacted the limitation. The

---

[2] Thomas I. Emerson, *Towards a General Theory of the First Amendment*, New York: Random House (1952).

[3] Part 1 of the Constitution Act, 1982, being Schedule B of the Canada Act 1982 (U.K.), 1982, c. 11 (hereinafter, Charter).

Alberta Press Act and the Quebec Padlock Law, both enacted in 1938, are probably the two most notorious examples of this.

But as the law giveth, the law also taketh away. Constitutional rights are no exception. None of the fundamental freedoms enumerated in Section 2 of the *Charter* are absolute. Freedom of the press is not an unfettered right. The limitation is set out in Section 1, which qualifies the rights in Section 2 by stating, "The *Canadian Charter of Rights and Freedoms* guarantees the rights and freedoms set out in it subject only to such reasonable limits prescribed by law as can be demonstrably justified in a free and democratic society."

As a result, and regardless of how important freedom of expression is in a democratic society, there are times when it must give way to other rights in the name of some greater social good. This means that under some circumstances freedom of expression and the press can be proscribed as long as the limitation can pass the three tests set out in Section 1. In other words, freedom of the press must compete in the judicial marketplace with other guaranteed rights. It is a balancing of rights in the pursuit of other social goals, such as the protection of reputation, privacy, social groups and morals; the administration of justice, including fair trial; not to speak of national security. Sometimes those rights are seen as more important than freedom of the press, to the utter dismay of journalists. But the picture isn't quite as bleak as free press advocates sometimes make out. Journalists win as many cases as they lose.

As a result, many laws—some would say too many—are in place to complicate the work of the journalist. These can be found in the *Criminal Code*, other federal acts and a variety of provincial legislation, such as libel and slander acts. They can also be found in the common law, law that has escaped codification and exists in judicial precedents. The most outstanding example of this, for the journalist, is contempt of court.

For journalists, the law is a two-edged sword. In Canada, it empowers them to pursue their craft vigorously and fearlessly but it can also throw up roadblocks that may get in the way of getting that important story. The trick, of course, is to know the law and use it to one's advantage. Know what the limitations and boundaries are. One of the first duties generally for any journalist is to stay out of legal trouble. It's not much fun going to jail or paying a fine for contempt of court or having to mortgage your house to pay libel damages.

Though some may chafe under the burden the law imposes on the journalist, it has to be remembered that freedom of the press doesn't exist in a vacuum. Other rights and freedoms are as important to others as freedom of the press is to journalists. Understanding the balance will lead to better journalism and a healthier society.

That is the aim of this chapter. It is by no means an exhaustive survey but an overview that flags some of the more common legal pitfalls that journalists encounter as they go about their business serving the public interest. Its purpose is to serve as an introduction, to enable journalists to recognize potential legal trouble and deal with it before it becomes a serious legal problem.

The law of defamation

There probably is a no area of media-related law that is more important for the journalist than defamation. It presents a most vexing problem because it is so little understood by many journalists. Defamation law seeks to preserve the reputation of individuals, who can sue if they think their reputation has been attacked in a publication. That necessarily leads to a limitation of other rights, such as freedom of the press, because the media can't just say anything they please about other people without some legal justification. Defamation law, then, is a balance of rights: reputation on the one hand and freedom of the press on the other.

Defamation simply means lowering an individual's reputation in the eyes of other people in the community. It is an umbrella term that encompasses two kinds of defamation: slander and libel. Slander is a defamation for which there is no record. That is, a conversation between two or more people that disparages the character of an individual or individuals is a slander. Libel is defamation in any permanent form that has been "published," or made known to other people. A slander can easily become a libel if it is written down or taped then "published" to other people. Permanence can take many forms: newspapers, books, magazines, records, CDs, even graffiti on a wall. Defamatory radio and television broadcasts are considered libels, as are postings on the Internet, because there is a record.

Defamation is a provincial jurisdiction and is contained in the various provincial and territorial defamation acts. It goes without saying that every journalist should be familiar with the defamation act of the province or territory in which he or she is working. It is a civil wrong as opposed to a criminal offence. A civil wrong—called a tort—is a dispute between individuals; a criminal act is behaviour that is deemed to be contrary to the public good. There is a criminal version of defamation, called defamatory libel (S. 298), that is codified in the *Criminal Code*. It is rarely used, but journalists should be aware of its existence. In many ways, it is similar to civil libel but is different in one important respect. Though defamatory libel lowers the reputation of an individual in the eyes of the community, it also affects public order. That is what makes it a criminal offence. For example, publishing that someone is a child molester is a civil libel. Publishing that someone is a child molester and therefore should be tarred and feathered and run out of town may be prosecuted as a criminal libel because it may lead to a breach of the peace.

One of the most important aspects of Canadian libel law is that it is what is known as a strict liability tort (except in Quebec). That means that a plaintiff (the complainant) is entitled to succeed in his or her lawsuit even if there was no intent to harm or proof of negligence or fault on the part of the defendant. This has far-reaching repercussions for the media. For example, having made an inadvertent error or an honest mistake that unintentionally libeled someone is no excuse. In Canada the media take responsibility for everything they publish, and they are accountable for it in law.

This also means they are responsible for what their sources tell them. If a journalist publishes libelous information or comments provided by a source, the journalist and the publisher take responsibility for the publication. The claim that you are just quoting someone else is not a defence. The source, if he or she is identified, can be sued, but so can the journalist and everyone else involved in the publication of the offending material.

As a result, it is absolutely imperative that journalists, before they write anything derogatory or negative about someone, are so sure of the facts that their publication will not lead to a lawsuit. After all, the primary objective should be to avoid law suits, not just be able to defend yourself successfully. Law suits tend to be expensive. This is especially important because the court will assume without proof that the plaintiff has suffered injury to his or her reputation and is entitled to damages.

The situation is somewhat different in Quebec, where the

plaintiff must prove fault on the part of the journalist and that his or her reputation was damaged as a result. There must also be some relationship between the libel and the damages sought.[4]

The plaintiff's case

To succeed in an action for libel, the plaintiff must prove three things: that the offending words were published, that he or she was identified or at least identifiable and that the offending words are defamatory in law and in fact.

Proving publication is generally the easiest. All that is required is a copy of the publication and proof that it was seen by at least one other person besides the plaintiff and the defendant. But the scope of the publication affects damages. The more widespread the publication, the higher the damages are likely to be. In other words, publication in a magazine or newspaper that has a circulation of 3,000 limited to a certain areas is likely to result in lower damages than in a national publication with a circulation of 300,000.

This, of course, raises the spectre of Internet publication. May damages be affected by publication in a small local newspaper or magazine if it posts the offending material on its Web site where it can potentially be seen by millions of people? Quite likely, although no cases so far have addressed this particular issue.

But a recent decision by the Supreme Court of Australia demonstrates a development in this regard. In an unprecedented ruling it decided that an Internet posting is published wherever it is read, not where it originates. Normally a publisher is sued where the business in incorporated or

---

[4] Michael G. Crawford, *The Journalist's Legal Guide*, 4th Edition, Scarborough, ON: Carswell (2002).

where he or she has commercial interests. In this case the Internet magazine was published in the U.S. and had only a handful of readers in Australia, where the publisher had no commercial presence. Nevertheless, the court allowed a Melbourne businessman to sue the publication in Australia, under Australian libel law. If widely adopted internationally, the ruling has enormous implications for Internet users. It means that they could be sued in any country or jurisdiction where their material is read.[5]

Because defamation protects individual reputation, the plaintiff must be the person defamed and must be identifiable to other people in the community. If the plaintiff is not named, it is enough if others can recognize the plaintiff and know whom you are talking about. Plaintiffs may be both natural persons (individuals) and legal persons, such as a business or a corporation. But no one may sue on someone else's behalf. Only the person who claims to have been defamed can sue. The husband of a politician can't sue on his wife's behalf. And the husband can't sue because he has been emotionally affected by the libel of his wife, but not directly defamed himself.

These requirements have two other important consequences. The dead can't be libeled and neither can large groups of people where individual identification is impossible. Reputation dies with a person and no one may sue on behalf of a deceased person, no matter what you say about him or her. The only time a living person may sue in relation to a publication about someone who is dead is if the living person is also libeled as a result. Writing that the surviving wife of a deceased suspected spy aided and abetted her husband's illegal activities is a libel of the spouse, not the dead husband.

---

[5] Owen Gibson, "Australian court in landmark ruling," *The Guardian* (U.K.), Dec. 21, 200.

She can sue; he can't (for obvious reasons).

Group libels are a thorny question. Two provinces, Ontario and Manitoba, have provisions in their statutes that allow groups of people to sue. But at common law and in other provinces and territories, only identifiable individuals can sue. That means that if the group is so large that specific individuals within it can't be identified, there can be no case. Small groups of people are another matter. If the group is so small that it affords identification of everyone in the group, then each individual can sue.

A classic example of this occurred some decades ago when a newspaper columnist published a column in which he called members of a jury murderers after a young man had been convicted of murder and sentenced to death. Some members of the jury sued, even though they had not been identified by name in the column. But the group was small enough that people in the community knew about whom he was talking and identification was established. The jurors won.

Establishing defamation is somewhat more problematic. The judge must first be satisfied that the words complained of are capable in law of being defamatory. This is a subjective test that seeks to establish whether other people in the community, once having read the words, might think less of a person. In trying to determine the effect of words on the general public, the judge takes into account a number of considerations, including the context in which the words were published and the social and political mores of the time. Some allegations—criminal conduct, sexual impropriety and immoral behaviour—are, on their face, always capable of being defamatory. Other allegations depend on interpretation in the context of the times. In some instances, what was considered libelous 20, 30, 40 or 50 years ago may not be so today.

For example, being called a communist may have been highly defamatory at the height of the Cold War and, in fact, led to some libel cases. Today, given the current political climate it is unlikely that being called a communist would be seen as overly pejorative. That is where the general population comes in. The judge must consider the plain meaning of the words complained of and the effect they may have on ordinary men and women in the community. The test is what the effect is on the general population, not special interest groups. For example, being called a racist would not likely be demeaning in the eyes of the other racists. But the general community will likely have a different reaction.

A journalist must be prepared for legal consequences if he or she publishes stories about a person's professional misconduct or incompetence in a person's trade or business, financial irresponsibility or disgraceful or unusual behaviour. Claiming that a person is seriously ill or is poverty stricken when he or she is not, is also potentially libelous. These are called "Red Flag" allegations.[6]

If the judge decides that the publication is capable in law of being defamatory, the jury must then decide whether the words are in fact defamatory of the plaintiff. It does so based on the evidence presented in court and the defences raised by the defendant. If it finds for the plaintiff, it will award damages to be paid by the defendant. If it finds for the defendant, the case is dismissed.

The plaintiff may also choose to try to prove malice on the part of the defendant, but this is not a requirement. Malice means more than ill will or spite. In libel law it means the misuse of a public interest for personal gain or other ulterior motives. Serious consequences ensue for the

---

[6] John J. Watkins, *The Mass Media and the Law*, Englewood Cliffs, NJ: Prentice-Hall (1990).

defendant if there is proof of malice. For one, the defendant is no longer entitled to use the defences of qualified privilege or fair comment. Both defences allow the media to publish defamatory statements in the public interest as long as certain conditions are met. (More on this later.) The misuse of those defences for purposes other than for which they were intended is considered malice. Malice is established by evidence about the conduct of the defendant. If proven, it also results in punitive damages. This is compensation in excess of actual damages and may be considered a kind of punishment to the defendant.

Besides the assumption of damage once the plaintiff's case has been established, the court also assumes that he or she has a good reputation, that no one has the right to damage that reputation and that the defamatory allegations are false.

It is now the defendant's turn to rebut these assumptions and justify the publication by raising a legally recognized defence. Given the burden of proof on the plaintiff, some claim that the deck is stacked unfairly against defendants because they have so much more to prove.

The defendant's case

The defendant can rely on four defences to justify the publication of the alleged libel: truth, consent, fair comment and qualified privilege. Only one of these requires him or her to prove the truth of the libel. The other three allow the defendants to escape liability if the words are libelous, as long as certain conditions are met.

Truth and consent are absolute defences because they can't be negated by proof of malice. The exception is in Quebec, where the defence of truth must be accompanied by proof of public interest. In other words, even if a defamatory statement is proven true, it will still lead to damages if there is no proof it was published in the public interest.[7]

Consent simply means that plaintiff has given the defendant permission, directly or indirectly, to publish the libel. On its face, this defence appears absurd. Who would give anyone permission to publish libels about him or her? The fact is that it doesn't have to be that direct. Consent is established if the plaintiff knowingly speaks for publication to the defendant about the libelous matter. But for this defence to be viable there has to be some discussion on the record about the libelous matter at hand. "No comment," or a simple "It isn't true" is not permission and doesn't entitle anybody to publish the libel and then plead consent.

The usefulness of this defence is also limited by the fact that it can be used only by those to whom consent was actually given. It cannot be passed on by the defendant to others and cannot be used by those who overheard, but did not participate in, the conversation or interview. In other words, a publication that "scalps" a newspaper article about an interview with a politician that contains libelous information about that politician cannot rely on consent for a defence if it is sued. The first newspaper got the consent, the second didn't.

Truth imposes a heavy burden but it is the perfect defence if all defamatory allegations—the sting of the libel—are provably true. This includes both facts and any defamatory conclusions that flow from those facts. This is not always easy. Facts may be relatively easy to prove but that can't always be said of the conclusions we draw from these. Consider the statement "He is despicable because he was convicted of stealing a loaf of bread." Proving that someone was convicted for stealing a loaf of bread

---

[7] Gerald A. Flaherty, *Defamation Law in Canada*, Ottawa: The Canadian Bar Foundation (1984).

is relatively simple. Proving the conclusion that he is despicable because of it rather less so. Perhaps he stole the bread because he had to feed his hungry children. Is he still despicable?

Truth is probably the least understood of the defences. It cannot be used, as some seem to believe, to simply support an honest belief in the information presented or to report a libelous rumour. If you report that someone is an arsonist and he sues you, you can't rely on the defence of truth simply because someone told you and you honestly believed it to be true. It may be true that someone told you or that a rumour exists, but that doesn't prove the truth of the sting of the libel—which is that someone is an arsonist. If you claim that someone sets fires and you use truth as a defence, you must prove by direct evidence that the plaintiff is an arsonist. Hearsay and rumour are not good enough.

The same may be said for defamatory innuendo. Sometimes it is not what is said but *how* it is said or what is *not* said that results in a libel. For example, if an article about cheating on university exams indicates that one particular student doesn't cheat on Tuesdays because of religious beliefs, the implication is that he or she cheats every other day of the week. Similarly, comparing a person to Rasputin carries an innuendo and may lead to a libel action.

As a result of its onerous nature, truth is not often used as a defence. The defence of choice is fair comment, one of the public interest defences. And for good reason. It actually allows journalists to publish libelous comment or conclusions about a set of facts—provided the facts underlying the conclusion are provably true. This is an exceedingly broad defence that allows the media to publish libels in the public interest as long as the publication meets certain conditions:

❑ the defamatory allegations must be comment or conclusions, not statements of fact

❏ they must be based on facts clearly identified in the publication or well enough known in the community so they don't have to be repeated

❏ there must be an honest belief that the libel is true

❏ the publication must be in the public interest

❏ there must be no malice

A word about "fair." Interestingly enough, fair simply means that, being in possession of the same facts, others in the community could come to the same conclusion. In other words, the conclusion must be consonant with the facts. If it is, the conclusion drawn from them is fair as long as any person could make it. The conclusion need not be reasonable or one that many or, indeed, anyone agrees with. It can actually include comments that most people would consider unreasonable and unfair.[8] Hence, fair seems somewhat of a misnomer. Fair implies reasonableness, but here it simply means that if the conclusions are to have any legal weight they must be based on true—and provable—facts. In other words, conclusions based on falsehoods can't be fair.

These requirements, of course, include headlines and photo captions. These are all part of the overall package. A libelous headline or photo caption that is not supported by the facts in the story cannot be defended with fair comment, much less truth. Headlines and captions must be consonant with the facts and must not exaggerate or go beyond these. Summaries and interpretations of facts in stories for headlines and captions must accurately reflect what the story says. A headline or caption may be libelous even if the story is not.[9]

Qualified privilege is another public interest defence and

---

[8] Flaherty, *Defamation Law in Canada.*

[9] *Tedley v. Southam Co.* [1950] 4 D.L.R. 415 (Man. K.B), in Crawford, *The Journalist's Legal Guide.*

is predicated on the belief that under certain circumstances the media should be allowed to report libelous information without fear of being sued. But the circumstances are limited to certain occasions and governed by a set of rules. Unlike a member of Parliament, for example, the media never have an absolute privilege.

The privilege defence generally protects the media from being sued for reporting libelous information in the following circumstances (these may differ slightly from province to province):

❑ proceedings of Parliament, legislatures and their committees

❑ public bodies that derive their authority from Parliament or a legislature

❑ proceedings of professional or trade associations that exercise authority over their members

❑ lawful meetings held for the purpose of discussing a matter of public concern

❑ synopsis of reports, bulletins, notices, etc. issued for the information of the public by Parliament, etc.

❑ findings or decisions of associations relating to their members

❑ judicial and quasi-judicial proceedings

And for the journalist to claim qualified privilege as defence, the report must satisfy the following requirements:

❑ It must be a fair and accurate report. It doesn't have to be verbatim but must reflect the substance of what went on in a reasonably balanced way. In other words, a story about a meeting in which only one side of an argument was reported could not be said to be fair and accurate.

❑ There must be no comment by the journalist. This defence

protects reportage only. It cannot be used to defend libelous commentaries, editorials or opinion columns.

❏ The meeting or proceedings being reported on must have been open to the public or information available to the public. This doesn't protect private gatherings or leaked information.

❏ There must be no malice.

❏ In the case of judicial proceedings, the report must be contemporaneous with those proceedings. The information must have been heard in open court by judge and/or jury. This does not protect conversations overheard in the corridors or interviews with participants in the trial.[10]

As a result of this defence, the media may report on parliamentary, judicial and related proceedings without fear being sued. There is no obligation to attempt to establish the truth of what is being reported, which would be impossible in any case.

Although both fair comment and qualified privilege are public interest defences, it should be noted that there is no public interest defence *per se*. Except in Quebec. The Quebec *Civil Code* and several court decisions have established protection for people who, in the public interest, divulge information relating to the administration of public business or the conduct of public officials. In this the Quebec law reflects a 1964 decision in the U.S. Supreme Court relating to libels involving public officials. There is nothing comparable in the other provinces or territories.[11]

---

[10] *Libel and Slander Act*, R.S.O., 1990.

[11] Flaherty, *Defamation Law in Canada*.

Apologies and retractions

However broad the defences available to the defendant may be, it is inevitable that there may come a time when none of these will serve adequately, when, despite the best precautions, you were wrong or can't come up with the appropriate evidence to defend a libel case is court. What then? The wisest course of action under those circumstances is to retract and apologize. A retraction or apology will go a long way to mitigate damages in a case that can't be won. Though it doesn't extinguish the right of a potential plaintiff to sue, a retraction that sincerely apologizes for the libel will affect any damage award. For example, under these circumstances, the plaintiff is not entitled to punitive damages. Perhaps even more important, more often than not the plaintiff will be satisfied by this restoration of his or her reputation and drop the case. But apologies, to be effective and acceptable to a court, must fully retract the sting of the libel. They can't be half-hearted or flippant.

Protecting the administration of justice

Even though one of the cornerstones of the Canadian justice system is its accessibility and openness, much of the law that limits freedom of expression is informed by a perceived need to protect the administration of justice. More often than not this translates into the right to a fair and unprejudiced trial. For example, when a case comes before the courts, no one may interfere with due process. Hence, the courts have wide powers, both in statute and common law, to regulate reportage of judicial proceedings and even access to the courts and to evidence. These are often called "gag orders."

These restrictions often apply not just to the media but to the general public as well. For example, a judge may exclude people from the court in the interests of justice. Sometimes the restrictions apply to more than the actual legal proceedings. Hence, the courts have seen fit at various times to ban books, plays, films and television documentaries if the subject matter deals with a case that is before the courts. For example, a Red Deer, Alta., judge banned the staging of a play in Calgary that dealt with Nazi death camps, an issue that was the subject of a trial in his courtroom. This was to prevent prejudice against the accused by those—especially jury members—who might have seen the play or been exposed to publicity about it.

The underlying reason for these laws is to prevent due process from falling into disrepute, the assumption being that a legal system that isn't respected will not be trusted to dispense proper justice. In considering freedom of expression and the press in relation to judicial proceedings and the Canadian legal system, it is evident that the practices of a free press often conflict with such legal issues as fair trial. The issue is often referred to as trial by media.

So far, Canada has escaped the excesses of the American system, in which an accused is often presumed to be guilty in the media before any trial has taken place. This is because of the laws that place restraints on the reportage of trials and other matters involving justice. Much of this law is intended to preserve the notion that trials and other judicial proceedings are decided on the evidence presented in open court in front of judge and jury, not by outside influences, such as the media, which are not restrained by evidentiary rules and other such niceties. These restrictions affect not just the reporters who cover specific trials from day to day, but also columnists, editorial writers and those who write about larger legal issues that may arise out of specific trials. Journalists who ignore the rules may face contempt of court charges or criminal charges as outlined in the statutes.

All of this clashes, of course, with our cherished traditions of an open court system. "Where there is no publicity, there is no justice," Jeremy Bentham said long ago. Indeed, the *Charter* states that everyone has the right "to be presumed innocent until proven guilty ...in a fair and public hearing...." But it is also generally accepted that when presumption of innocence and fair trial clash with the open court principle, it sometimes becomes necessary to limit access.

Statutory prohibitions

These are generally reasonably well-defined laws that limit access to the courts or place publication bans in very specific circumstances. For example, the *Criminal Code* prohibits publication of a whole array of evidence in sexual assault cases, including names of complainants and witnesses under 18 (S. 486). The court may also place bans on bail hearing evidence (S. 517) and on preliminary hearing evidence (Ss. 537, 539, 542).

Preliminary hearings are inquiries to determine whether there is enough evidence to send the accused to trial. It is not a trial itself. Only the Crown presents its case. As a result, the hearing is very one-sided and may present an unfair picture of the accused to the public and any potential jurors. To prevent prejudice, a ban may be placed on evidence presented. An automatic ban is placed on any confession or admission of guilt the court may hear, regardless of whether there is a ban on the rest of the evidence.

Another section (S. 648) bans publication of information and/or evidence in a trial that the jury has not heard and is not entitled to hear. In any trial, admissibility of evidence and other legal arguments may be a central theme. Generally the jury may not hear these legal squabbles or be exposed to publicity about them until the judge says they can. Until that time this information may not be published for fear that the jury will be exposed to it and become biased.

The new *Youth Criminal Justice Act*, which has replaced the old *Young Offenders Act*, is one of the more complicated statutes that deals with publication bans. More often than not, the statutes are fairly straightforward and clear as to what can be published and when. The same cannot really be said of the new youth justice act.

One of the central tenets of youth law is to protect the privacy of the young offender so that he or she can be more effectively rehabilitated. The old act placed automatic publication bans on any evidence that might identify the young offender. There was a minor exception in the case of suspects still at large who need to be identified to protect the public. But it was very limited and expired as soon as the suspect was in custody.

Though confidentiality is still the norm (S. 110[1]), the new act somewhat expands the circumstances under which a young offender can be identified. The most important of these for journalists is when a young offender is convicted of a "presumptive" offence but receives a youth sentence. The presumptive offences include first- and second-degree murder, manslaughter and sexual assault (Ss. 110[2][3][4]). But caution is advised: for example, in the public interest a judge may still place a publication ban on the identity of a youth sentenced for a presumptive offence. As well, identification may take place only after the youth is sentenced. In other words, a youth accused and convicted, but not yet sentenced, is still protected. Because the new act just came into force, its provisions are still untested.

Contempt of court

As the *Criminal Code* and other statutes protect very specific aspects of judicial proceedings, contempt of court is an umbrella common law that protects the administration of justice as a whole. It derives from an early English concept that if people are to have respect for the justice system, it must be seen to be fair and impartial and untainted by outside influences. "There cannot be anything of greater consequence than to keep the streams of justice pure and clear," Lord Hardwicke, Lord Chancellor of England, said in 1742.

Because it is a common law and uncodified, its application is often erratic and uneven. That presents a vexing problem for journalists. Media behaviour that is clearly in contempt of court often goes unpunished. At other times, in other places, similar behaviour *is* punished. What to do? When does the law apply and when doesn't it? The simple rule is that the law always applies but its use depends on those involved in a particular case. In other words, a contempt of court that goes unnoticed in one case may result in a contempt citation in another.

At the very least, every journalist should have a reasonably clear understanding of what contempt is in order to make informed decisions about what to publish and when. When a journalist consciously breaches contempt law, there may or may not be legal consequences depending on the circumstances of the case and the people involved. As one editor once told a reporter, "It's not whether you break the law, but whether you get caught."

Contempt of court consists of three categories: the *sub judice* rule, scandalizing the court and disobeying a court order (the last also exists as a *Criminal Code* provision). Contempt may take place inside or outside the courtroom. Punishment may involve fines and, sometimes, jail terms.

Sub judice

The *sub judice* rule exists primarily to promote and protect fair and unprejudiced trial. When a proceeding has come under the jurisdiction of the court, any act that interferes with the court's role in determining guilt or innocence is a breach of the *sub judice* rule and punishable with a contempt citation.[12]

It is a strict liability criminal offence because proof of intention to prejudice a trial is unnecessary, as is proof that anyone was actually prejudiced.

As the law has evolved, the rule has undergone some minor changes. Today it is generally accepted that there are seven ways to breach the rule:

- ❏ publishing confessions or admissions of guilt before they become evidence in the trial
- ❏ prejudging a case during the trial and before all the evidence has been heard
- ❏ urging a particular result before all the evidence has been heard
- ❏ abusing parties to an action
- ❏ publishing previous convictions or claims of bad character not in evidence at the trial
- ❏ publishing a photograph of an accused when identity may be an issue at trial
- ❏ reporting one proceeding in a way that may be prejudicial to another
- ❏ publishing the results of media investigations of a case that is still before the courts

Some of the rules are more important than others, but all are meant to protect jurors or potential jurors from being influenced by information they are not entitled to know about a case. In other words, the media should report only what has been said in open court in front of the judge and jury and is not the subject of a publication ban. This protects

---

12 Stuart M. Robertson, *Courts and the Media*, Toronto: Butterworths (1981).

the time-honoured principle that judges and juries make decisions about guilt and innocence based on evidence heard in court, not outside influences.

Timing and place of publication may mitigate a breach of the *sub judice* rule. Contempt law seeks to protect active trials. The more time that has elapsed between the trial and the breach, the less likely a prosecution. Similarly, publication of unlawful information in a magazine that is primarily read in Vancouver about a proceeding taking place in New Brunswick is unlikely to lead to legal consequences. That's because jurors or potential jurors are not likely to see it. That, however, may not apply if the magazine has a Web site, especially if there is evidence that it is widely read elsewhere.

Scandalizing the court

This category of contempt protects the dignity of the justice system. Scandalizing the court may be seen as lowering the reputation of the courts in the eyes of the public. For example, reporting a case, even if the trial is over, in a way that calls into question the court's impartiality and neutrality—hence, fairness—is a breach of this rule, as are claims that the justice system is biased against certain people or groups or is corrupt.

That doesn't mean the courts and the justice system are beyond scrutiny. There is nothing wrong with criticizing a decision on legal grounds. But the criticism must not impute improper motives.

An example of this is a case a number of years involving a well-known Toronto lawyer who, after losing a case, gave an interview in which he accused the courts and the police of sticking together like Krazy Glue. The implication was that the courts and police were in cahoots and nobody could get a fair trial no matter what the evidence. He was cited for contempt for scandalizing the court and barred from practicing law until he apologized. The conviction was eventually over-turned on appeal because some of the judges felt there was no intent to bring the justice into disrepute.[13]

Another famous case, in 1954, involved a Vancouver columnist who commented on the case of a 19-year-old man who had been sentenced to hang after being convicted of murder. The columnist had wanted to criticize capital punishment, a perfectly legitimate enterprise if he had only let it go at that. But he called the jurors criminals for punishing the man in such a manner and accused the judge of condemning him to "exquisite torture" for setting the date of execution so far into the future. He was cited for contempt and fined $250. The newspaper for which he worked was fined $2,500. It was pointed out to him that the jury had no role in the sentencing of the accused, which was required by law, and the date of execution had nothing to do with the judge being a torturer but to allow time for appeal.

The judge who fined the columnist and the newspaper said this: "To refer to the jurors in this case as criminals and to describe the judge as causing exquisite torture is calculated to lower the dignity of the court and destroy public confidence in the administration of justice...." This, he continued, must be stopped "in the public interest."[14]

The columnist, by the way, was also successfully sued for libel by some of the jurors even though none was named.

Court orders

Court orders take many forms and compel people to do something or not do something. For example, a court may

---

[13] The Canadian Press, "Lawyer wins contempt appeal," in *The Ottawa Citizen*, Nov. 28, 1987.

[14] Wilfred H. Kesterton, *The Law and the Press in Canada*, Ottawa: Carleton University Press (1984).

order a spouse to pay child support or order strikers not to picket a particular business. It may order witnesses to appear and testify in a court proceeding, or it may order a publication ban on the name of witnesses or certain evidence. It may order a journalist to reveal the name of confidential sources. Though court orders come in all shapes and sizes, disobeying a court order always leads to one conclusion: a likely contempt citation.

This category of contempt aims to protect the authority of the court and is a power the courts wield with more regularity than is the case with the other two categories. Though the use of the contempt power with respect to scandalizing and *sub judice* may be spotty and you may get away with breaking the rules, the same cannot be said of court orders. Any one who wilfully and knowingly disobeys the court will more likely than not, face a hefty fine or even a spell in jail.

Protection of sources

A word about revealing sources. Canada does not have shield laws that protect journalists from having to reveal the names of confidential sources under some circumstances. In other words, journalists have no *legal* right to promise such confidentiality.[15] They may do so on ethical grounds but this carries little weight when a court has determined that the name of the source is relevant to a legal proceeding and orders the journalist to identify his or her informants. The court does not always order journalists to reveal sources, but if it does journalists have no legal basis to resist such an order. If they do, they very likely will be held in contempt of court.

---

15 *Marilyn Moysa* and *The Labour Relations Board* et al, Supreme Court of Canada , 1989 (unreported).

Journalists should be especially wary of confidential sources that supply libelous information about other people. If the material is published and the journalist is sued, the court may demand to know the source of the information if the plaintiff claims malice on the part of the defendant journalist and the source. Because the concept of malice involves state of mind and motive, the court will not be able to rule on the issue if it does not know who the source was.

Obscenity, hate and blasphemy

Of all the criminal laws that pertain to freedom of expression, none is more problematic than those that deal with hate propaganda and obscene and blasphemous material. This is because such things as hate, obscenity and blasphemy are mostly in the eye of the beholder and are so poorly defined, defying Sir Thomas More's observation in *Utopia* that "If laws are not clear, they are useless."

The obscenity law (S. 163 [1–8]) is supposed to protect the morals of the community from being corrupted, and it encompasses all sorts of expression, artistic and otherwise. It defines as obscene "...Any publication the dominant characteristics of which is the undue exploitation of sex, or of sex and any one of the following subjects, namely crime, horror, cruelty and violence...."

A community standards test has evolved to determine the meaning of "undue exploitation." Though there is some leeway for artistic merit, the Supreme Court of Canada decided a number of years ago that "undue exploitation must be judged by the harm a community believes might occur as a result of people being exposed to it." It went on to say that "harm in this context means that it predisposes a person to act in an anti-social manner as, for example, the physical or mental mistreatment of women by men, or, what is perhaps debatable, the reverse."[16]

Note that the section says nothing about pornography. To be deemed obscene, a work need not necessarily be considered pornographic. This opens the door to including works that merely offend someone. The issue of child pornography is covered in another section of the *Criminal Code*.

The hate propaganda law (Ss. 318, 319) protects "identifiable groups" from harm. The *Criminal Code* defines identifiable groups as "any section of the public distinguished by colour, race, religion or ethnic origins." This definition, of course, ignores a number of communities, who have long since clamoured for inclusion in the law.

The law criminalizes advocating genocide, hate speech that is likely to lead to a breach of the peace, such as a riot or assaults on individuals, and statements that wilfully promote hatred. The first two prohibitions are not generally seen as a problem, even though activities such as incitement to murder are already dealt with elsewhere in the *Criminal Code*.

The third section is seen by many as the biggest problem because it criminalizes speech and ideas. The speech needs not have any other consequence than to offend someone who hears it. Hate is not defined. Hence, any speech deemed offensive by a group included in the definition might claim it has been subjected to hate and press for a prosecution. But prosecutions must have the consent of the provincial attorney general. As a result, the law is rarely used.

Blasphemy (S. 296) as law is even more problematic. It is covered in three short sections of the *Criminal Code*. It states that anyone who publishes a blasphemous libel is guilty of an offence and may go to jail for up to two years. Interestingly,

---

[16] *Butler v. The Queen*, Supreme Court of Canada, 1992.

it doesn't say what constitutes blasphemy, leaving it to the jury to decide on a case-by-case basis based on the evidence. In other words, blasphemy can be anything the jury says it is. This is a law that has fallen into disuse, not having been used for decades. But it's still on the books, so it's not exactly a dead issue.

Privacy

So far, the laws discussed are reasonably complete and recognized legal concepts. Although of some obvious importance to the journalist, privacy, again except in Quebec, is only vaguely protected in Canada. As a concept, what privacy experts have called "the right to be left alone" is not recognized in English common law. In other words, there is no tort of privacy. It must be created and protected by statute.

A good illustration of this is the famous case of a woman who went to use the bathroom while drinking in a rural Wisconsin bar. The owner followed her, kicked open the toilet door and snapped Polaroid photographs of her. She later saw him pass the photos around to other bar patrons. She sued but lost when the Wisconsin court said there was no right to privacy under common law. Wisconsin adopted a privacy law in 1977.[17]

Great Britain, too, now has a statutory privacy law by virtue of having had to incorporate European Union law into its legal system. Among the first to take advantage of the new law were the actors Catherine Zeta-Jones and Michael Douglas. They successfully sued an English magazine for invasion of privacy after it published photographs of their wedding without permission. Before 2002 that would have

---

[17] David Johnston, "Quebec law protects privacy; common law doesn't," *Southam News*, Sept. 27, 1997.

been impossible.[18] Except in Quebec, that is still impossible in Canada. This means it is perfectly legal to publish photographs of people without their permission without fear of being sued. The photos may be evidence of another unlawful act, such as trespass or disrupting a religious service, but can't be used to sue for invasion of privacy.

The absence of a common law statutory tort of privacy has resulted in a somewhat confusing array of federal and provincial privacy and privacy-related laws.

Federal privacy laws protect information about individuals that is held by the government, government institutions and the private sector from falling into the wrong hands. Federal acts such the *Criminal Code* are of more immediate relevance because they contain provisions that are privacy related and specifically protect "the right to be let alone."

These include the unlawful interception of private communications by electronic or other artificial means—in other words, communications that can't be heard naturally; trespass at night; disrupting a religious service; and various publication bans pertaining to sexual assault complainants and witnesses in sexual assault cases.

Already mentioned, the *Youth Criminal Justice Act* protects the privacy of young offenders except in special circumstances.

Most provinces have established privacy acts of one kind or another that protect their residents from being harassed or intimidated, but all offer protection for the journalistic enterprise. For example, the Saskatchewan *Privacy Act* specifically exempts journalists: "An act, conduct, or publication is not a violation of privacy where it was that of a person engaged in a news gathering for any newspaper or other paper containing

---

[18] Frances Gibb, "Zeta-Jones wins historic privacy case," *Times of London*, Dec. 21, 2000.

public news, or for a broadcaster licensed by the Canadian Radio-television Telecommunications Commission to carry on a broadcasting transmitting undertaking, and such act, conduct or publication was reasonable in the circumstances and was necessary for or incidental to ordinary news gathering activities."[19]

The situation is somewhat different in Quebec, which probably has the most far-reaching privacy laws in the country. Articles 35 and 36 of the *Civil Code* specifically protect privacy without limitation: "Every person has a right to the respect of his reputation and privacy."

In 1988, a 17-year-old Montreal woman sued a Montreal literary magazine for publishing, without her consent, a photograph of her sitting on the doorstep of a building. She was awarded $2,000 in damages. In 1998, the Supreme Court of Canada upheld the award saying that Quebec privacy includes the right to control the use of one's images, even if a photo is "in no way reprehensible" or has not injured the person's honour or reputation.[20]

That doesn't mean that in Quebec the media can't ever publish people's photographs without their permission. In trying to protect freedom of the press, the court also said the right of the public to be informed sometimes takes precedence over the right of privacy. It listed seven such circumstances, including photographs of persons engaged in public activities, persons who appear incidentally in a photograph of a public place, such as a building, or persons in a group photograph in a public place if they are not the principal subjects, such as a demonstration.

Other provincial statutes also protect the privacy of specific individuals. All provinces have child welfare legislation

---

19 R.S.S. 1978, c. P-24.

20 Stephen Bindman, "Ruling supports privacy rights," *Ottawa Citizen*, April 10, 1998.

that prohibits identifying children who are caught up in the legal system. These prohibitions don't just include names, but all information that might identify them indirectly.

The absence of privacy rights has other far-reaching implications. For example, it allows the media to "out" people living anonymously in the community who have been convicted of serious crimes, often at serious risk to their safety.[21]

Canadian Radio-television Telecommunications Commission (CRTC) regulations also have something to say about privacy. Though you don't need permission to record telephone interviews or conversations to which you are a party, consent is need by all those taking part to broadcast all or part of the tape.[22]

Copyright, the Internet and intellectual property issues

Before the Internet, copyright was a reasonably straightforward proposition. Your journalistic, literary or artistic creation belonged to you and if someone stole it from you or in some misappropriated it as his or her own you could sue for copyright infringement.[23]

For example, if your story was read word for word on the radio without credit, that was a copyright violation. If you taped a radio broadcast and printed it word for word in a magazine or newspaper without credit, that was a copyright violation. It still is, of course. And if it were just a matter of a newspaper or a radio station pirating your material, the issue would be pretty simple.

---

[21] Klaus Pohle, "Convicted, jailed, released – and hounded," *The Globe and Mail*, Toronto, May 23, 1997.

[22] Crawford, *The Journalist's Legal Guide*.

[23] *Copyright Act*, R.S.C. 1985, c C-42.

Copyright applies, among other things, to any original writing, music, lyrics, photographs, drawings, maps and charts, whether published or unpublished. It attaches automatically to the work the moment it is created. Contrary to popular belief, there is no need to officially register the work or publish it to establish copyright.[24]

It is important to note that events, news and ideas cannot by copyrighted. It is the format in which these are presented that is protected. For example, a news conference by the prime minister cannot be copyrighted. What is subject to copyright law are the reports of that news conference on radio, TV, newspapers, the Internet and elsewhere.

But that doesn't mean that journalists can never use other people's work in their own stories. Probably the most important exemption from copyright law is what is known as "fair dealing."[25]

"Fair dealing" allows journalists, for purposes of review and criticism and news reporting, to quote from another person's work without infringing on copyright as long as it is properly attributed. The act doesn't quantify "fair dealing" but it is generally accepted that the excerpts must be brief and the reason for their inclusion in your work clear. The difficulty, however, is that there are no hard and fast rules as to what "brief" means.

Though the act focuses on copyright, it also established what are called moral rights.[26] These protect the integrity and original form of the work even if the copyright has been sold. This is particularly important for editors. They have to be aware that substantially editing or rewriting a work without express permission will violate the author's moral rights.

[24] Crawford, *The Journalist's Legal Guide.*

[25] *Copyright Act*, Ss 29-20.2.

[26] *Copyright Act*, S. 14.1 (1).

Another violation of moral rights is the use of the material for purposes other than that for which it was sold. For example, a photograph purchased to illustrate a magazine or newspaper article cannot be used later in an advertising campaign without permission. Essentially, this gives journalists, freelance or otherwise, important control over how their work is edited, reworded or otherwise used.

Unfortunately, the same can't be said once your work is posted on the Internet. Just as other laws that regulate conventional publications apply to the Internet, so do copyright laws. The Internet is not some lawless free-for-all marketplace of information. People have been sued, been held in contempt of court and charged with various criminal offences for their Internet postings. The issue is not regulation but enforcing the regulations.

The issue of enforcement has significant implications for the freelancer who sells one-time publication rights to a story or photograph to a magazine or newspaper. Before the Internet, this was a pretty simple proposition. It appeared once and that was the end of it. Any subsequent publications could be easily monitored. Nowadays, however, the publisher is more likely than not to demand permission to also put it up on a Web site, where it might stay for years. The benefits to the publisher in such an arrangement are obvious, just as are the disadvantages for the freelancer.

To mitigate these disadvantages, many freelancers are asking for agreements that place strict limits on the length of time that a story can remain on the publisher's Web site. After that time the story is deleted.

Unfortunately, that's probably not enough. Once on the Internet, the story can be read, downloaded, replicated and reposted on potentially dozens of other Web sites anywhere in the world—all unbeknown to its creator. If, as a result, others purloin your story as their own, you may never know. Or if you do find out, you may be able to do very little about it, short of suing. In other words, direct control over the material is lost, no matter what precautions have been taken. Short of coming to an agreement with a publisher not to post your story on a Web site, which is highly unlikely, this may be part of the cost of putting up with global information technology.

A final word

Freedom of expression and of the press are in a delicate balance. The legal system seeks to regulate that balance. This is but an introduction to and an overview of some of the laws that restrain the media in the pursuit of some larger societal good. Every responsible journalist should be conversant with the laws that affect his or her pursuit of information. Indeed, the courts have made it amply clear that they expect a high standard of care from journalists.

The criminal law is reasonably easy to follow because it applies everywhere in Canada. Provincial statutes that regulate or have an impact on the media vary widely and are not so easily digested because there are so many of them. Nevertheless, every journalist worth his or her salt should have at least a cursory understanding of the laws of the province in which he or she is working. Only by understanding the law as it pertains to them can journalists maximize their freedoms while also being responsible citizens.

Selling Your Story

Hannah Moor said she thinks anyone can write one saleable manuscript. "Any adult has lived enough that they have something in their life they could write about. Even if they need a lot of editorial help," she added. "But how they go about it from there will tell whether they're a writer or not."

There are a variety of approaches. Going to journalism school will give you the greatest opportunity to hone a variety of skills—from print to broadcast. However, it also requires the greatest commitment of time and money. David Harris, editor of the *Presbyterian Record*, recommends starting out in mainstream journalism, if possible. "Valuable lessons can be learned there," he said. "Everything from writing styles to meeting tight deadlines to how the world of journalism works—researching and interviewing."

However, perhaps you're not in a position to go to journalism school. And as to getting experience in the mainstream press, well, today, most media outlets want journalism graduates—people who can hit the ground running, people who don't need any training in how to write a lead or structure a story.

But this isn't an "all or nothing" situation. Workshops and

courses can be extremely helpful and are increasingly available—including excellent ones offered within the Christian community. Every year The Word Guild, an association of Canadian writers and editors who are Christian (http://www.thewordguild.com/home.html), organizes the two-and-half-day God Uses Ink writers' conference in Guelph, Ont., with writers, editors, publishers and agents on the faculty. Inscribe Christian Writers' Fellowship, another national writers' organization (http://www.inscribe.org/), holds a fall conference in Edmonton and a spring WordShop in Calgary. Both organizations offer some regional one-day seminars. Both organizations also offer membership benefits that you might find useful in networking and in fostering your growth as a writer.

Perhaps one of the best tests of whether you are a one-story person or someone with a developable talent is this: Deep down within, do you have an urge to write? A corollary of that is to ask yourself, "Do I want my writing to be read by others?" Harold Jantz, founding editor of *ChristianWeek*, said, "The truth is, I have a hard time not expressing myself in writing. I wake up in the middle of the night and I'm composing sentences. Something is trying to get out."

The challenge is in getting those words out in a form that editors will accept and that will ultimately engage readers. Earlier chapters addressed many of the elements necessary for crafting and writing good stories. In this chapter, we'll examine how you might attract the attention of an editor—the first, and most essential, step in getting your stories published!

The basics

If you think you haven't yet developed a nose for stories, then go back and reread the chapter on story ideas. This should help you deal with one of the major problems Doug Koop, editor of *ChristianWeek*, confronts on a regular basis.

He said a major failing of would-be writers is that "they don't understand the different arms of journalism [reporting and commentary]. And most often," he added, "they don't know what news is. The result is a lot of story proposals that are basically testimonials or personal commentary."

Understanding the difference between news and commentary will help you avoid a problem David Harris commonly sees—that is, interjecting personal views into a news story. "Writers need to reflect on not allowing their faith perspective and political views to colour the story itself," said Harris. "This is perfectly acceptable, of course, if they're writing a column. But for news, they have to set their own feelings aside and let opponents of their personal position speak. It's essential that they be scrupulously fair. And," he added, "that they let the story speak for itself."

Clarifying the different forms of writing found in the Christian publications you want to write for will help you shape your story ideas.

Koop flagged another problem area. He said beginning writers tend to think that if they've had something published, that automatically must mean it was good. "So, they assume that if you write something, then you'll want to publish it," he said. Unfortunately, as he pointed out, having a single article published doesn't necessarily mean it was good. But the experience *can* create unreal expectations. It may set people up for disappointment. Perhaps they don't realize how much work is required to get something to the publishable stage—to say nothing of the work involved in getting their idea accepted in the first place.

Joe Sinasac, editor of *The Catholic Register*, said he works hard to educate people "about what the paper is aiming for, and what we're dealing with. We are a national newspaper," he said. "We don't do things out of church basements any more. We want sophistication."

Story ideas

If you think you can approach an editor and say, "I'm a writer. What do you suggest I write about?" then you probably won't get very far. Editors have one of the hardest jobs in the business. They're responsible for the overall editorial content and direction of their publication. This means they've got to have a handle on the big picture. But it also means they've got to be hands-on, concerning themselves with the most picayune detail. In other words, trying to interest, attract and keep readers is as much a part of their job as checking the shortest story for accuracy. Coming up with story ideas for unknown, would-be writers is not high on their list of priorities.

However, they are *always* on the lookout for new talent, for writers who can be cultivated to provide good, strong copy on a regular basis. Getting their attention and becoming an integral part of their stable of writers means the ball is in your court; you have to come up with good, strong story ideas.

"Fresh ideas," said Rick Hiebert, editor of *Testimony*. "If people want to tell the same old story, then don't suggest telling it in the same old way. I want fresh approaches—especially to Christmas and to Easter. I also like to encourage analysis," he added. "Also, writers need to be willing to address different topics from a broad range of perspectives. And struggles don't always have to be presented in a positive light. We need stories where someone is struggling with a real difficulty and although it didn't turn out well, that person has a positive outlook."

Kenn Ward, former editor of *Canada Lutheran*, said the kind of material submitted to him tends to fall into two camps—Christmas and the death of a loved one. "While I do accept one of these kinds of stories every now and then, the writer really needs to bring a fresh angle," he said. Speaking in the same vein as Hiebert, Ward said he looks "for creative approaches and fresh ideas."

To one degree or another, every Christian publication tries to present stories that help people think through their faith. For Ian Adnams, editor of *The Canadian Lutheran*, this means story ideas "have to be real and touch people where they're at."

Whatever you want to write about, make sure you expend your marketing energy on coming up with a story idea—not on writing the story. There's little point in submitting a manuscript for publication if you haven't been given the go-ahead from an editor. Yes, perhaps an unsolicited manuscript might be selected for publication. However, this is risky. It might just as easily be rejected, in which case you may have wasted a lot of time working on something that will never see the light of day.

Instead, put your energies into coming up with an idea you can pitch to an editor. If the editor doesn't like it, he or she may be able to suggest a way to rework it. Or, a worst-case scenario, the rejection will have saved you the grief of investing in an unpublishable piece of work.

If the editor does like it, then it means your subsequent story will be all the better. You'll have had the benefit of the editor's feedback on the idea, as well as suggestions for ways to sharpen your focus and find research sources.

Research, research, research

Having just said you shouldn't invest a lot of time in writing a story "on spec" (i.e. without having been given approval from an editor), there are some things you should *definitely* take the time to do. You won't regret it, as time invested in this stage will pay off down the road.

First, don't even think about sending a story idea to an editor without knowing something about that publication.

What type of publication is it—a newspaper or a magazine? What types of stories does it tend to run—features, analysis, news? Who is it aimed at—church leadership, youth, a specific denomination or a general Christian audience?

To get a sense of the scope and variety of Christian publications, check out the membership directory of the Canadian Church Press. It provides a sense of each publication's mission, as well as contact information. You'll find the directory of member publications on the Internet (http://www.canadianchurchpress.com/).

In addition, find out whether the publication you're interested in has a set of writing guidelines. Many do, and reading them carefully can also save you a lot of grief. *The Catholic Register, ChristianWeek* and *Faith Today*, for example, are just some of the Christian publications that provide such guidelines. Read them *before* you contact the editor. Though most editors would be happy to discuss a concrete story idea with you, they don't have the time to fill you in on the basics—the kinds of things any serious writer should have found out independently (and which indicate you have fundamental research skills).

Guidelines usually cover such things as the publication's mission statement, the kinds of stories editors look for, the types of writing style, length of articles, payment policy and submission guidelines (where and how to send in story ideas, and in what format).

Though this may not be possible with all editors, Patria Rivera, editor of *Catholic Missions in Canada*, also suggests talking to the editor in advance of sending in an idea. "Find out what kinds of stories the editor would like to have," she said. "By reading the magazine you see what kinds of stories they run. Then again, perhaps the editor would like to focus on others—but they aren't visible yet. Talking to them gives you a chance to explore what direction they might want to go in."

Also, go back in time. Read back copies of the publication you're interested in writing for. One of the worst things you can do is to suggest a story idea on a subject that the publication covered within the past year.

Though reading and studying the publication will give you a good sense of its aims and objectives, you're also going to need to find out as much as you can about the readership. Harold Jantz, founding editor of *ChristianWeek*, advises writers to "be alert to the world in which the readers live and within which they must live out their faith. I see this as extremely important," he said. "We have been called by God to live whole lives in a world of much brokenness and pain, much conflict and sorrow. Christ entered our history to bring redemption to such a world. That should be known by these writers and they should be prepared to address the issues that raises."

Take the time to research your story idea. Don't make the mistake of proposing a story about something that may later turn out to have no substance. You *must* do enough advance research to be able to suggest and support a specific story, not merely a topic.

This means being able to provide the editor with a story focus as well as the names of people you would interview and supporting documents you might research. It also means being able to answer the So what? question. Why is this story important? What relevance does it have to the readership of this publication? Why should people care about it?

Ted Schmidt, editor of *Catholic New Times*, put it this way: "You *must* know your story. It must go through you and be who you are." In addition, he thinks it's important that people who write for the Christian press "have a theology that's deep and not pie-in-the-sky or fundamentalist." And, he added, "they should be well read. People send me stuff and it's horrible."

Pitching an idea

The query

The best way to contact an editor is to send a query letter. This isn't a job application. It's a straightforward note in which you pitch your story idea. This means being clear and to-the-point. State your focus, include research information as well as sources, and describe why the story matters.

If you're an unknown writer to the publication, tell the editor why you are qualified to write this story. And include any samples of previously published articles.

Be brief. Be polite. And make sure you include contact information!

Write well

When you send in your story idea, you're not just presenting a proposal. You're also giving the editor a taste of your writing skills. So check—and double check—that your copy has no typos or grammatical errors. Write clearly and simply. Make sure your material is organized in a thoughtful and logical way.

Above all, don't write in clichés. Editors want people who can write simply but also with originality.

Hannah Moor said she thinks the writing in the Christian press has improved significantly from when she first started to write 50 years ago. "I think there are more intelligent people writing now," she said. "Maybe there are more intelligent editors, too."

Think art

Editors have to think in terms of the big picture. They know that art matters because it matters to readers. In fact, it's often what attracts them to read a story. So whatever photographs or illustrations or charts can accompany a story are important to them. Think in those terms at every part of the journalistic process. When you are researching, be on the lookout for good illustrations, diagrams or charts. When you're interviewing someone, think in terms of photographs. But think much broader than "head and shoulders" shots. Such photographs can be deadly. Instead, think of the kind of setting they could be photographed in, that would best express who they are and what they do.

This kind of attention to detail will endear you to editors and help improve your observation skills.

Examine your motives

So you think you want to write. What's more, you think you want to write for a Christian publication. But do you have any idea why? Joe Sinasac said people often approach him and say, "I want to do something for the church." Though he said he appreciates the positive intention behind the sentiment, it isn't necessarily something that will translate into good writing.

"I'm hesitant when I hear that," said Sinasac. "I want people with something deeper. People who are seekers of the truth, seekers of understanding—not just looking to 'help the church.'"

Just reading a certain type of story can raise a red flag for Jantz. "If I read something that has no life about it," he said, "or that doesn't try to catch people's interest or is self-absorbed or doesn't connect, then, to me, that writer should ask themselves: 'Is this what I really ought to be doing?'"

Keep reading good writing

When you aren't coming up with story ideas, researching, writing and reworking your stories, then read a wide range of good writers. That's a good way to pick up on techniques that work as well as ones that don't. The better you get at discerning the difference, the better you'll become at applying what you've learned to your own writing.

Don't get discouraged

Being rejected is difficult. There may be a perfectly good reason why your story idea wasn't accepted. But it can feel very personal. Or you might have your story idea accepted, write the story, and then be told by the editor that it needs work. Lots of work. In fact, you may be asked to start again from scratch.

Muriel Duncan, editor of *The United Church Observer*, said not to get discouraged. "Sometimes people just have to look at this kind of thing as a learning experience, especially if a lot of rewriting is involved," she said. "But they need to know why it happened. We're willing to work with new writers if they show promise and a willingness to rework their ideas."

She added that just because a couple of story ideas are rejected doesn't mean you should throw in the towel. "People might hit deterrents, but I say, 'Keep sending in those queries and persevere.' Perseverance is a good thing."

Marianne Meed Ward adds her voice to the "Don't get discouraged" theme. And when she says it, she means it in two ways. First, don't get discouraged if your story idea is rejected, or your writing needs reworking. For her, it comes with the turf.

Second, though, she refers to the ways in which writers can become discouraged about covering an issue, especially if the people you need to deal with aren't keen that the story be published. In that case, they may put up roadblocks. "I've heard it all," said Meed Ward. "People might say, 'This isn't a story.' Or they might accuse you of 'fear mongering.' You have to have a thick skin to be in journalism. But you have to have an even thicker skin to be in religious journalism because you are a part of the community you're writing about."

Like Muriel Duncan, Doug Koop advises beginning writers to think of both the rejections and the discouragement as learning experiences. "It takes time to learn," he said. "And it involves a lot of practice."

Don't forget to have fun

Much of this book has stressed the hard work of researching and writing. But if that were all it is about, then most of us wouldn't have devoted our lives to it. In fact, there is tremendous joy to be had in doing this kind of work. There's the excitement that comes from coming up with that "fresh approach," that original story idea.

There's considerable satisfaction to be had in the sleuthing required to track down sources and in doing the hard research. You come into contact with a wide range of people—people you'd probably never have the opportunity to meet otherwise. And the things people will tell you! It is both a blessing and an enormous responsibility to be the repository of people's dreams and horrors.

Honing your writing skills brings a particular pleasure. Finding your voice, for example, is a lifelong quest. And getting feedback from readers—especially those who say, "What you wrote really made me think," or even, "It changed my life," makes all the hard work worthwhile.

Ted Schmidt is convinced that anyone who does this kind of work "must have tremendous love and enthusiasm for what they're doing. You've got to have the enthusiasm to change the world and make it a better place," he said. "But you should have a good sense of humour and not take yourself too seriously."

Ian Adnams would add a strong "amen" to Schmidt's last sentiment. To him, too much of religious writing is what he calls, "earnest journalism." "To me, there's got to be a joy in writing," he said.

Harold Jantz has been a writer and editor since the 1960s. He said he's never regretted turning his back on the teaching career for which he'd been professionally trained. Instead, he's given his life to the crafting of articles and stories that can help people in their faith journey. "I loved it right from the start," he said. "It's enjoyable and satisfying, and I felt I could contribute through it. I feel privileged I was able to do it."

Appendix A:
Practical Tips

Think of this chapter as a resumé—a reminder of all we have discussed in detail earlier. Use it as a quick guide to effective research and writing.

Finding story ideas

❑ Read, read, read—everything. Explore *everything* that's out there. Determine how it relates to your audience and the mandate of your publication.

❑ Talk to a lot of people. Put yourself in situations where you'll meet people from a variety of walks of life and from diverse communities.

❑ Listen, listen, listen.

❑ Keep a notebook to record observations, overheard conversations and ideas.

❑ Track what's going on in your life and in the lives of those around you.

❑ Watch and listen to broadcast news. Make connections between what is going on and the experience of your community.

❑ Throw away nothing that might be remotely useful. Keep everything well filed.

❑ Organize a tracking system for sources—people you can phone periodically to keep yourself up-to-date on developments and issues pertinent to your readership.

❑ Use the McKercher/Cumming Q–S–A formula to test a story idea. Do you have question that needs answering? A source that can answer it? An audience interested in the answer?

❑ Work on developing several story ideas at a time.

Identifying news

The McKercher/Cumming acronym is SIN: significant, interesting and new.

News values

❑ timeliness—something is happening now

❑ impact—the more people affected, the greater the news value

❑ prominence—the better known the person or institution, the greater the news value

❑ proximity—the closer to home something happens, the greater the news value

❑ conflict—between countries, organizations or people, or internally

❑ currency—relevancy

❑ necessity—material is considered important to your readership

❑ conciliation—introducing disparate parts of communities to each other

232

Basic elements of news

❑ answering the five Ws and H (Who? What? When? Where? Why? and How?)

❑ answering So what? Why should we care about this issue/event/person?

❑ including the elements of time, place, people and drama

❑ being fair, balanced, precise and accurate in every detail

❑ attributing statements and verifying facts

❑ seeking a diversity of sources and diversity of opinion within those sources

Thinking critically

❑ Ask probing questions.

❑ Search for evidence.

❑ Be willing to question assumptions, your own and those of others.

❑ Be open-minded about the material in front of you.

❑ Focus on what people do, as well as what they say.

❑ Examine and analyze *everything*.

❑ Expect to learn from your own stories.

Researching

Researching: The Internet

Internet sources can be problematic. If you're thinking about using material off the Internet then ask yourself the following questions:

❑ Who put the Web site together? What do you know about the knowledge base of the people who did it?

Can you reach them to confirm material on their site?

❑ If you can't get in touch with the originator of the material, is someone named on the site who can verify the information?

❑ Is it possible to tell when the page was posted, or when the information was written? How frequently is the page updated?

❑ How complete is the material? Are there any holes, any issues not covered?

❑ Is there advertising on the site? If so, is it clearly separated from the information?

❑ Rely on sites that are "official," e.g. Statistics Canada.

❑ Corroborate material you glean from the Internet (unless the source is impeccable, like Statistics Canada).

Researching: Documents

❑ Think about all the angles remotely associated with the focus, or theme, of your story and find related documents (newspaper clippings, books, research reports, royal commissions, magazines, journal articles, statistics).

❑ Take notes and/or photocopy relevant documents.

❑ Identify them correctly.

❑ Organize your findings ASAP.

Researching: Observation

❑ Be as unobtrusive as possible. Don't make yourself the centre of attention.

❑ Use all five senses.

❑ Watch for telling details about characters and their environment and about place.

❑ Attempt to understand the meaning of what you observe.

Interviewing

Sources

- ❑ institutional—people within a bureaucracy or institution, the authority figures
- ❑ human—people affected by a policy, decision or issue
- ❑ documentary—the people behind the records, books, reference works, newspaper clippings, the Web
- ❑ diverse—people representing a variety of opinion as well as diversity of age, gender, physical capability, ethnicity

Interview preparation

- ❑ Research your topic as thoroughly as possible.
- ❑ If possible, ask sources in advance of an interview to recommend material to help you prepare.
- ❑ Sketch out a list of the questions you'll need answered.
- ❑ Break that list down in terms of the sources who can potentially answer them. Take those question sheets with you to your interview.

The interview

- ❑ Identify yourself and the publication you're writing for; explain why you want to do the interview; make it clear that answers will be "on the record."
- ❑ Keep the interview as short as possible.
- ❑ Remember, a statement is not a question. Avoid long preambles and keep your questions short and simple.
- ❑ With rare exceptions, avoid questions that elicit a Yes or No answer.
- ❑ Take notes as well as tape the interview.
- ❑ Observe your surroundings as well as your source's

interactions with others, mannerisms and comfort level with questions.

❑ Give sources time to think about answers. Never rush them.

❑ Don't be afraid to ask sources to rephrase their answers in clearer language if they're answering in jargon.

Notes

❑ Always carry extra notebooks and pens or pencils.

❑ Keep your list of questions separate from the notebook that you're using so you don't have to flip back and forth.

❑ Develop your own personal shorthand to help you keep up.

❑ Put an asterisk beside any answers you want to come back to later in the interview.

Tapes

❑ Check your equipment before you leave to make sure everything is working and that you have everything you need.

❑ Take extra batteries and cassettes/mini-discs with you.

❑ Set the counter at 0 when you begin recording and "signpost" your notes from time to time to make it easy to find a quotation later without having to replay the whole interview.

Assertiveness

❑ Go the extra mile to glean that extra anecdote, that essential fact.

❑ At the end of an interview always ask a source whether there is anything else that should be discussed.

❑ At the end of an interview always ask a source to suggest

other sources or other research materials.

❏ Ask tough questions, but ask them with respect.

❏ By all means play the "devil's advocate," but make it clear what you are doing. Avoid aggressive questions based on your own biases.

❏ Save your hardest questions for last.

❏ Always attempt to get one more person to interview.

Sawatsky's seven deadly interviewing sins

❏ making a statement instead of asking a question

❏ asking double-barrelled questions (two questions at the same time)

❏ overloading questions (broad topic, little specificity)

❏ inserting remarks in questions

❏ using trigger words ("scandal," "junket," "conspiracy")

❏ exaggerating

❏ asking a closed question (requiring only a Yes or No answer).

Characteristics of good questions

❏ neutral

❏ short and simple

❏ open (but not open-ended):

- *what happened?*
- *what do you mean?*
- *how would you describe it?*
- *what was the turning point?*
- *why?*

In addition, *always* ask for anecdotes to illustrate points.

Attentive listening

- ❏ Ask a question.
- ❏ Listen for the answer.
- ❏ Follow up with a question.
- ❏ Look for body cues.
- ❏ Read the body cues.
- ❏ Use those markers to ask your next question.

Reporting

Finding your focus

- ❏ Remember that a topic is not a focus. To help you find your focus, ask yourself these questions:

  - *What's the story?*
  - *What surprised me the most?*
  - *What is the one thing my readers need to know?*
  - *What did I learn that I didn't expect to learn?*
  - *What information is absolutely essential?*
  - *Is there one anecdote or quotation that illustrates what this story means?*
  - *Is there an image that sticks in my mind?*

- ❏ Write a focus statement using a subject, active verb and "because." (Someone is doing something to someone. Something is happening to someone for a reason. Note: Those are possible focus statements. But a focus doesn't require that someone be at the receiving end.)
- ❏ Write a draft headline.
- ❏ Write a draft lead.
- ❏ Write a draft nut graf.

- ❑ Write a draft conclusion.
- ❑ Tell the story to a friend to see, in the telling, what focus emerges.

Organizing

- ❑ Transcribe your notes as soon as possible after an interview.
- ❑ Write down your observations ASAP.
- ❑ Organize your research material thematically.
- ❑ Highlight essential passages of interviews and documents.
- ❑ Organize the essential passages according to your focus.
- ❑ Draft a story structure.

Writing

Essential components of a story

- ❑ accurate information
- ❑ anecdotes (to illustrate key points) backed up by concrete facts
- ❑ credible sources
- ❑ proper attribution
- ❑ a strong point of departure
- ❑ engaging and relevant quotations judiciously placed
- ❑ fairness and balance (of sources and in writing)
- ❑ clean copy following the style requirements of your publication
- ❑ succinct, clear and energetic writing
- ❑ showing, not telling
- ❑ having every detail, fact and quotation on focus

Attributions

❑ when you didn't personally witness a situation or event

❑ when the source of information requires identification

Writing tricks

❑ Develop discipline. Set a target for how much you're going to write each day or how long you'll spend writing each day. Then stick to it.

❑ Witness yourself at work. Where are you procrastinating? What excuses keep you from setting down your thoughts?

❑ Tell yourself you're just writing a draft, not an award-winning story.

❑ Post inspirational verses beside your computer.

❑ Write about the things you see, hear or think. It's good practice.

❑ Think of yourself as a writer, then apply yourself to your work like a professional.

Writing tools

❑ Keep a dictionary, thesaurus, *The CP Stylebook* and reference materials beside your writing area.

❑ If you write on a computer, have a good backup system and use it regularly.

News (inverted pyramid story structure)

❑ All the essential information is contained right off the top. A one-paragraph lead (of perhaps one or two sentences) sums up the story.

❑ Details are presented in descending order of importance.

Features (hourglass story structure)

- ❏ The structure is like two pyramids whose points meet in the middle.

- ❏ The top part contains all the information of an inverted pyramid.

- ❏ The middle, a.k.a. the turn, signals that a narrative is about to begin.

- ❏ The final part (the narrative) contains details and background information.

Nut graf story structure

- ❏ An anecdotal lead is followed by sections that amplify the story's focus.

- ❏ The nut graf follows the anecdote. It runs anywhere from one to three or four paragraphs and summarizes the focus.

- ❏ The nut graf tells readers what the story is about and connects the anecdote to what follows.

Profiles

- ❏ Of people. Make readers *see* the person (using observation skills), *hear* the person (using quotations), *know* the person through a variety of sources—the person being profiled, family, friends, co-workers, people who've been touched by the person, even detractors and, of course, the environs.

- ❏ Of institutions. Make readers see the building or organization, feel how it touches people, hear how it operates and understand what it does. Once again, use a wide variety of sources.

Obituaries

Be sure to include

- ❏ correct spelling of the person's name, title, occupation and address
- ❏ date, place and cause of death
- ❏ birthplace and date of birth
- ❏ survivors
- ❏ funeral arrangements
- ❏ anecdotes and recollections of family, friends, co-workers
- ❏ memberships, activities or accomplishments
- ❏ contextual social history, if applicable

Editorials

- ❏ Construct them carefully to interpret, explain or appraise an event or issue.
- ❏ Challenge readers to further thought or debate.
- ❏ Choose a timely topic.
- ❏ Base your case on knowledge.
- ❏ Write clearly and write well.

Commentary

- ❏ Express your personality.
- ❏ Write from a position of strength—i.e. do your research. A column is no excuse for intellectual laziness.
- ❏ Support your position.
- ❏ Write clearly and write well.

Leads

- ❏ Do not write more than 30–35 words.

❑ Decide whether you're going to provide all the essential information in the lead or delay it with an anecdote. If the former, make the focus clear in the lead.

❑ Use concrete nouns and action verbs.

❑ Attribute if required.

Revision

❑ Think positively. Revising is an essential part of producing good stories.

❑ If possible, let some time elapse between writing your draft and beginning to revise.

❑ Put on your editor's hat and pretend it isn't your work you're critiquing.

❑ Be brutal. Cut out all clutter and all material that isn't on focus.

❑ Ask tough questions.

- *Does the lead work?*
- *Is the story on focus?*
- *Are the five Ws and H addressed?*
- *Is everything signposted?*
- *Do the quotations, facts, sentences and paragraphs work together seamlessly?*
- *Are all my words concrete and specific?*
- *Are the verbs active?*
- *Am I being direct?*
- *Am I staying on focus?*
- *Am I using plain language?*
- *Have I incorporated description about the things I observed?*
- *Have I varied the length of sentences?*
- *Does my story follow a logical progression?*

- *Did I signpost where I'm going and how I'm going to get there?*
- *Is everything as clear and accurate as possible?*
- *Did I write conversationally?*

❑ Check for accuracy.

- *Names. Are place names and proper names correctly spelled?*
- *Telephone numbers and addresses. Has contact information been verified?*
- *Event-based stories. Are times and places correct?*
- *Numbers. Have numbers and statistics been verified?*
- *Photos. Is everyone properly identified?*
- *Facts. Have they been corroborated and/or verified?*

Fallout from a controversial story

❑ Ensure that your research is beyond reproach.

❑ Listen respectfully to those who dispute your findings.

❑ Point concerned readers to places where they can voice their reaction—letters to the editor, an op-ed column.

❑ If they reveal a new angle on the story you've written, try to arrange to write a follow-up article.

Mistakes

❑ Admit a mistake immediately and take corrective action. An apology and a written retraction in the next issue of your publication is a good beginning.

❑ Learn from them. Double-check everything you write from thereon in. One mistake could be chalked up to being a novice. Another one would mark you as unprofessional and your work as untrustworthy.

Being ethical

For ethical decision-making ask

❑ What are the issues?

❑ What are the relevant facts?

❑ What are the possible courses of action?

❑ What are the likely consequences of those actions? For example, weigh the positive and negative impact (the negativity directed toward an institutional policy, say, as opposed to the public's need, and right, to know).

❑ What course of action should I take?

Selling your story

Before the query

❑ Research the publication you're interested in writing for.

❑ Check out its Web site. If it has a set of writers' guidelines, read them.

❑ Read previous editions of the publication. From this, you'll get a sense of its preferred writing style and types of stories.

❑ Research your story idea.

❑ Make sure you are researching something with a focus, not exploring a vast topic.

The query

❑ Address it to the managing editor or editor unless instructed to do otherwise.

❑ Make it succinct and to the point.

❑ Explain what the story is, who your sources are and

why the story would be of interest to that publication's readership.

❏ Explain who you are and why you are qualified to write the story.

❏ Include samples of previously published work (clippings).

❏ If you've never been published, write the story on spec, so the editor can get a sense of your capabilities.

❏ Remember that the query is a sample of your writing. Check, then double-check, for accuracy and plain, clear writing.

Follow-up

If you said in your query, that you'd check back within a certain a period of time, then do it.

Characteristics of a good feature writer

❏ the ability to connect with a wide variety of people
❏ curiosity
❏ a keen sense of observation
❏ a good knowledge of the language
❏ an appreciation of the power of the written word
❏ the ability to organize and synthesize immense amounts of material
❏ the ability to write relatively quickly
❏ a well-read mind

Characteristics of a good journalist

❏ curious

- ❏ intelligent
- ❏ open-minded
- ❏ hardworking
- ❏ persistent
- ❏ knowledgeable
- ❏ fair
- ❏ compassionate
- ❏ reliable
- ❏ honest
- ❏ courageous

Appendix B:
Useful URLs

It's worth bookmarking the following sites. They are chock full of excellent information and resources.

CANADA NEWSWIRE:
http://www.newswire.ca

THE CANADIAN ASSOCIATION OF JOURNALISTS:
http://www.eagle.ca/caj/

CANADIAN CHURCH PRESS:
http://www.canadianchurchpress.com

INSCRIBE CHRISTIAN WRITERS' FELLOWSHIP:
http://www.inscribe.org/

JOURNALISMNET:
http://www.journalismnet.com/

JOURNALISM.ORG:
http://www.journalism.org

PERIODICAL WRITERS ASSOCIATION OF CANADA:
http://www.pwac.ca/

THE PEW CENTER:
http://www.pewcenter.org

THE POYNTER INSTITUTE:
http://poynter.org/

SOCIETY OF PROFESSIONAL JOURNALISTS:
https://www.spj.org/

SOURCES:
http://www.sources.com/

THE WORD GUILD:
http://www.thewordguild.com/home.html

Glossary of Journalistic Terms

Analysis

An informed, intelligent and reasoned assessment of the issues involved in a news story. Not a judgment call, an analysis contains a logical ordering of perspectives based on interviews with a wide variety of sources and careful thought. By putting the news in a much broader context, analysis adds depth and meaning. (In the words of the *CP Stylebook*, "the analysis builds a structure of interpretation upon a foundation of factual material.")

Assignment

A story allotted to a reporter from his or her editor.

Attribution

The source of information in a story identified by name (and title). Attribution is required when the reporter did not witness the event she or he is writing about and when the information expresses an opinion or value judgment.

Background

This term is used in three ways. It can refer to the body of knowledge a writer accumulates through time. It can refer to material written into a story to provide context about an event or circumstance. Finally, it can refer to material a source provides, but doesn't want attributed to him or her. This material may or may not be used in a story, depending on the agreement made with that person.

Backgrounder

A particular type of story that "provides historical context, sets out the whys and wherefores of a complicated issue in the news, explores legal questions or lists the pocketbook impact of the development under review" (*The CP Stylebook*).

Beat

An area (such as religion or education) assigned to a particular reporter to cover on an ongoing basis.

Byline

The writer's name, usually placed above the published story.

Checking the clips

Doing background research on an issue, event or person by reviewing previously published newspaper articles on the subject.

Clippings/Clips

Published stories.

Column

A signed article of opinion.

Contempt of court

An act or omission tending to obstruct or interfere with the orderly administration of justice or impair the dignity of the court or respect for its authority.

Context

Information in a story that clarifies the relationships between the main characters, and between characters and their social, economic and physical environments, past and present.

Copy

The written form in which a news story or any other kind of journalistic story is prepared.

Correction

A printed retraction correcting a serious error. If the error is libelous, then it is always corrected immediately—often in a separate news story, rather than in the standard box assigned to corrections.

Correspondent

A reporter who files stories from a location outside the newsroom.

Cover letter

A letter that introduces you to a prospective employer. It is usually accompanied by your resumé and clippings.

Cutline

The descriptive or explanatory material that runs under a picture.

Deadline

The time at which copy is due.

Defamation

Something that harms the reputation of an individual (legal or natural) in the eyes of other people in the community.

Diversity

A component of effective reporting. It involves making a concerted effort to reflect the varied nature of one's readership—age, gender, race, for example. It also refers to including a variety of perspectives on an issue or event.

Draft

A version of a story. Not the final, revised (and polished) copy.

Edit

The process whereby an editor goes through the reporter's copy with a fine-tooth comb checking for accuracy, clarity, balance and inconsistencies in style. Editors suggest improvements to writers and expose holes in the story which they ask the writer to fill. If necessary, they shorten copy.

Editorial

An article of comment or opinion that reflects the official position of the publication. Commonly run on the editorial page, it is usually unsigned.

Exclusive

A.k.a. a scoop. A story a reporter has obtained that no competitor has.

Feature

A story that emphasizes the human aspects of a situation or issue. Features can also revolve around news. In that case, they have more content and context than a straight news story.

Focus

The central idea, or theme, of any piece of journalistic writing. A focus statement has a subject doing something for a reason.

Graf

Slang for paragraph.

Hard news

Event-based stories, such as an organization's annual general assembly or a fatal Sunday school bus accident. It also refers to depth coverage—stories that explore issues.

Head/Headline

Text that runs over a published story.

Head shot

A head and shoulders photo of a person.

Hourglass story structure

A story structure that provides the news values of the inverted pyramid, but the storytelling ability of the narrative structure.

Inverted pyramid story structure

A story structure that puts the most important, or newsworthy, information at the top and orders the rest in descending order of importance.

Investigative reporting

Using a variety of research and detective methods to unearth material that sources often do not want exposed. It often revolves around unearthing wrongdoing in the public sphere. However, investigative reporting can simply involve a complicated story that requires painstaking research, perseverance and imagination.

Journalism

A public act that involves reporting and commenting on news and current events. It is governed by established principles.

Kicker

A reward for readers who finish a story. A kicker doesn't sum up, provide a moral to the story or express an opinion or judgment. It might be a quotation, an image, a spark of humour, or an idea. Whatever, it should round off the story.

Kill

To decide not to run a story—ever.

Kill fee

The payment, usually a percentage of the original negotiated fee, that a publication pays the writer when it kills an assigned story.

Lead

The beginning of a story. Its objective is to "hook" the reader into reading through to the end.

Libel

A defamation that is "published" in any permanent form. Libel includes a defamation that is broadcast.

Masthead

That part of the publication that lists the publisher, editor and staff.

Morgue

The place where a publication's clippings from previously published articles are filed.

News

Information that is "significant, interesting and new," a definition coined by Carleton professors Catherine McKercher and Carman Cumming. There are many definitions of news, most of which involve the words "new," "interesting," "timely."

News judgment

The ability to recognize and report news of interest and importance to your readership.

News values

The attributes considered necessary in an event or situation to make it newsworthy. When making a news judgment, many editors regard timeliness, impact, prominence, conflict, currency and necessity as essential news values.

Not for attribution

A term describing information that can be used on condition that the source not be identified or be identified only in a general way. For example, "A spokesperson from the diocesan headquarters said…"

Nut graf

A paragraph (sometimes even two or three) that summarizes the theme of a story for readers. It usually follows an anecdotal lead.

Obituary

A published report of someone's death. It should include biographical information.

Off the record

A term meaning that nothing a source says can be used in a story, even if the source isn't identified. However, if the same information is given by another source *on the record*, the off-the-record information can serve as a second source for the purpose of verification.

On the record

A term implying that anything a source says in an interview can be used with attribution. Information given on the record allows readers to assess its quality because they know its source.

Op-ed page

Short form for the page opposite the editorial page. It is usually devoted to opinion columns.

Paraphrase/Indirect quotation

An accurate summary of what a speaker said, written in the reporter's own words.

Partial quotation

Only a part of what someone said, but still the exact words. Used for authenticity, emphasis, tone or credibility.

Plagiarism

Intentionally, or knowingly, passing on someone else's work as your own.

Press release

An announcement conveying a key message that its source would like published. It usually provides contact information and potential interview sources.

Profile

A story that paints a picture of someone by blending dialogue, action and description. This is done through unearthing background material, interviewing the person being profiled as well as the person's family, friends and associates, and observing that person in action.

Proof

The final layout of the publication reproduced on paper so corrections can be made before being sent to print.

Quotation

The exact words the person said or wrote. Quotations are enclosed between opening and closing quotation marks.

Reporting

Using a variety of techniques to collect and communicate information—interviewing, observing, note-taking, researching and analyzing, writing and broadcasting.

Resumé

A summary of a person's achievements, education, skills and work experience.

Retraction

A printed correction retracting a serious error. If the error is libelous, then it is always corrected immediately—often in a separate news story, rather than in the standard box assigned to corrections.

Rewriting/Revising

The key to a good story. Making changes to a draft to improve it in every way—sharpen the focus, tighten the writing and eliminate clutter.

Sidebar

A short, snappy collection of information (facts, figures, biological information) boxed for display. The information might be displayed through graphics. Sidebars always contain information related to but not found in the body of the main story.

Slug

A labelling line that gives an editor essential story information—the author, the category it falls into, the topic. It may also indicate whether there is any accompanying art.

Slander

Defamation for which there is no record (for example, a conversation).

Soft news

A story that involves something of casual, rather than critical, human interest. Soft news can have a news peg.

Source

Someone who has information, or can confirm information, that a reporter/writer can use for a story or for background.

Stringer

A freelancer who is on regular assignment with a publication.

Style

a) The unique way a reporter writes. b) The rules for capitalization, punctuation and spelling that establish consistent usage. *The Canadian Press Stylebook* is most frequently used in Canada for periodicals.

Subhead

Usually a one-line head (sometimes two) inserted in a long story at regular intervals to guide the reader through the content, recapture lagging attention, break up dense blocks of type or provide emphasis. The type is generally bold.

Tear sheets

Published stories.

Trim

To cut parts of a story, either for space considerations or to tighten the writing.

Update

To provide information to keep readers abreast of news related to an ongoing story.

Verification

Another word for checking the facts. The first form of verification is direct observation by the writer herself or himself. The second form is statistical data, documents, reports, books. The third form of verification is getting confirmation of details from a range of people who were there.

Vet

Another term for "edit." Also used for a review/approval process for a specific purpose, such as vetting by the legal department to ensure that a piece contains nothing libelous.

Wire services

A syndication service paid for by membership subscription.

News is gathered from a team of in-house reporters to serve a multitude of outlets. It's a utility, one-size-fits-all news service.

Bibliography

Arnold, George T. *Media Writer's Handbook* 3rd ed. Boston: McGraw Hill, 2003.

Bindman, Stephen. "Ruling supports privacy rights." *Ottawa Citizen* (April 10, 1998).

The Canadian Press, "Lawyer wins contempt appeal." *The Ottawa Citizen* (Nov. 28, 1987).

Crawford, Michael G. *The Journalist's Legal Guide*. 4th ed. Scarborough: Carswell, 2002.

Emerson, Thomas. I. *Towards a General Theory of the First Amendment*, New York: Random House, 1952.

Flaherty, Gerald A. *Defamation Law in Canada*. Ottawa: The Canadian Bar Foundation, 1984.

Gibb, Frances. "Zeta-Jones wins historic privacy case." *Times of London* (Dec. 21, 2000).

Gibson, Owen. "Australian court in landmark ruling." *The Guardian* (Dec. 21, 2002).

Johnston, David. "Quebec law protects privacy; common law doesn't." *Southam News* (Sept. 27, 1997).

Kesterton, W.H. *A History of Journalism in Canada*. Toronto: McClelland & Stewart, 1967.

Kesterton, Wilfred H. *The Law and the Press in Canada*. Ottawa: Carleton University Press, 1984.

McKercher, Catherine, and Carman Cumming. *The Canadian Reporter* (2nd edition). Toronto: Harcourt Canada, 1998.

Mencher, Melvin. *News Reporting and Writing*. 9th ed. New York: McGraw Hill Higher Education, 2003.

Milton, John. *Areopagitica*. 1644.

Norris, Kathleen. *The Cloister Walk*. New York: Riverhead Books, 1996.

Pohle, Klaus. "Convicted, jailed, released—and hounded." *The Globe and Mail* (May 23, 1997).

Robertson, Stuart M. *Courts and the Media*. Toronto: Butterworths, 1981.

Scanlon, Christopher. *Reporting and Writing: Basics For The 21st Century*. Fort Worth: Harcourt College Publishers, 2000.

Serrin, Judith and William (eds.). *Muckraking: The Journalism That Changed America*. New York: The New Press, 2002.

Strunk, William, Jr., and E.B. White. *The Elements of Style*. 4th ed. Boston: Allyn and Bacon, 2000.

Tasko, Patti (ed.). *The Canadian Press Stylebook*. 12th ed. Toronto: The Canadian Press, 2002.

Tasko, Patti (ed.) *Caps and Spelling*. 15th ed. Toronto: The Canadian Press, 2000.

Watkins, John J. *The Mass Media and the Law*. Englewood Cliffs: Prentice-Hall, 1990.

Winokur, Jon (ed.). *Writers On Writing*. Philadelphia: Running Press Book Publishers, 1990.

Zinsser, William. *Writing Well*. 6th ed. New York: Harper Perennial, 1998.

Index

A

Aboriginal Healing Foundation Fund, 43

about/almost/approximately/around, 142

Accept/except, 143

Accuracy, 82, 175–176, 239, 244, 246, 254

Active voice, 130–131

Acts 17:11, 59

Adjectives, 128

Adnams, Ian, 29, 125, 161, 163, 222, 229

Advice/advise, 143

Advocacy, 19

Affect/effect, 142

Altogether/all together, 143

Among/between, 144

Amount/number, 144

Analogy, 129

Analysis, 172, 251

Analytical stories, 85

Anecdotes, 35, 85, 107, 128–129, 138, 237, 239, 242

Angle, 100

Anglican Journal, 31, 42, 45, 75, 84, 133, 134

Anonymity, 60, 62, 169–170

Apology, 201

Areopagitica, 185

Art, 226

Assignment, 251

Attribution, 82, 233, 239, 240
  copyright and, 215
  definition, 108, 251
  objectivity and, 233
  permission for, 169

plagiarism and, 175

position of, 135

of secondary sources, 167

variations, 131–132

B

Background, 260

Backgrounder, 260

Bad news, 30–31, 75–76, 80

Balance, 82, 239

Ballard, Father Brian, 168–169

Beat, 260

Bentham, Jeremy, 209

Bereans, 59

Between/among, 148

Bias, awareness of, 18, 155, 178, 207, 237

Bird, John, 110

Bird, Roger, 86

Blasphemy, 210, 211

Body of the story, 115–116

Boucher, Sister Marie Claire, S.C.S.H., 112

Brackets, 136

Byfield, Ted, 78

Byline, 260

C

Canada Lutheran, 28, 55, 83, 91, 125, 136, 162, 222

Canada NewsWire, 249

The Canadian Association of Journalists, 257

Canadian Church Press, 180, 224, 249

The Canadian Lutheran, 29, 111, 125, 161, 223

The Canadian Press Stylebook, 133, 139, 140–144, 261

Canadian Radio-television Telecommunications Commission (CRTC), 221

The Canadian Reporter, 33, 77

Carleton University School of Journalism Code of Ethics, 177

The Catalyst, 57

Catholic Missions in Canada, 102, 163, 224

Catholic New Times, 32, 159, 225

The Catholic Register, 28, 76, 92, 111, 131, 156, 168, 224

Central idea, 100, 255

Characterization, 135–136

Charter of Rights and Freedoms, 186

Checking the clips, 37, 252, 255

ChristianCurrent, 78, 110

ChristianWeek, 29, 97, 99, 122, 159, 220, 224, 225

Chronological structure, 102–104

Citizens for Public Justice, 57

Clark, Roy Peter, 104

Clear writing, 126–128

Clippings/clips, 252